The First Term Through Poetry

The Trump Chronicle

Irvin R. Brookstein

Copyright 2020 Irvin R. Brookstein

The First Term, Through Poetry
The Trump Chronicle

All rights reserved.

No part of this book may be reproduced, transmitted, or stored in any form or by any means, mechanical or electronic, without permission from the publisher.

Email: ray@rayraypoetryworld.com

Author photos by Gasen, Miami Fl
Cover design by Martin Buchan, London England
Interior Book Design by Anamaria Stefan, Romania

. . .

Foreword

It's been said that every historical movement needs a poet. Whether you agree with it or not, the shocking 2016 election victory of Donald Trump, was clearly a result of a movement not seen before in recent political history.

Pundits worldwide were shocked. The political elite ruling class were stunned. Democrats across the country sat in disbelief on election night. Tears flowed, that the first woman candidate, Hillary Clinton, was denied her moment of glory. It was a crushing defeat.

As a Poet, I sat there on Election Night, and realized that this event would have immense significance worldwide.

That realization hit me like a ton of bricks. I was overwhelmed with the thought and a deep desire that I needed to poetically chronicle this Presidency, year by year, for as long as it lasts; With the potential of two terms.

What I did not anticipate, was that he would be mocked, challenged, investigated and impeached, by the full force and power of the House of Representatives, combined with the highest echelons of the intelligence community. The mainstream media would be completely allied with both of them as well.

All of these efforts over the First Term have failed to remove Donald Trump from office. So far the will of the People has survived.

Normally we see history recorded in the form of an encyclopedia, novels, videos, film, song and stage plays.

It's rare to see a history recorded in poetic form, because it requires the poet to track the events like a journalist or diarist, so that the poems can be creatively and chronologically connected. This became my goal on that November night when Trump was elected.

I wanted there to be a permanent "History through Poetry" for each year of his Presidency; The good, the bad and the ugly.

As a result, I have written and published three books, year by year; known as "The Trump Chronicle" Each year and each book stands on its own.

This Book, "The First Term, Through Poetry" combines selected poems from each year forming four Chapters. I tried to include the best of the best with the assistance of my creative team.

This is one of very few works I have been able to identify historically, that records poetically, any of the previous Forty-Four Presidential terms.

This Four-Year project, has taken me and many other Americans through twists and turns which we may never see again in History.

It combined joy and sorrow and every Human emotion in between. The events never ceased. I can't remember even one day of peace.

I felt an obligation and a duty to do my part, by writing these works, so that my own children and grandchildren, friends, family and any reader can always possess a permanent record of this historic period in History. This is my legacy.

Acknowledgment

I wish to recognize and thank the following individuals for their dedication, friendship and their contributions, which made this project possible:

Irene Peduto, NJ, selections of Poems.

Marlene Keener, KY, Market placement strategy

Teddy Selby, FL. Technology consultant, website design strategist, Web Master

Marie Bianco Blair, Lincoln, NE, editing

Michelle Sass, Fullerton, CA. Primary creative consultant in all aspects of the book strategy, design and publishing implementation.

My Mother, Estelle Brookstein, North Miami Beach, FL, for her love and motherly support and guidance.

Love,
Ray

Irvin R. Brookstein

Biography

. . .

Irvin R Brookstein, aka RayRay, is an American born author and poet. He was raised in New York and Ivy League educated. Over the past six years, Ray has distinguished himself as a Social Media phenomenon, showcasing his poetry on all the major platforms. He has also self-published several poetry books which record "History Through Poetry". His widely acclaimed "Trump Chronicle" poetically recounts The First Term. His energetic four year project is a very unique journalistic accomplishment. His style is rhythmic, versatile, compelling, and easy for all ages to read and understand.

"In Memoriam"

William W. "Hillbilly" Wilson, Jr. 1964-2020
R.I.P. Dear Friend

You could always read my poetry better than I!

Table of Contents

Chapter One
Year One

Election Night 2016 — 24

Ground Zero — 26

And the Ban Plays On — 29

ICBM — 30

The Battle Begins — 32

Once Upon a Time — 34

The Press Conference — 36

The Roast — 38

Speech to Congress — 40

Y R Taps — 42

Slip Sliding Away — 44

Sorrow in Manchester — 46

American Pastime	48
Patriot	50
Baby Boomer Amends	52
Rewriting History	54
Disgrace and Offend	56
Impeach This	58
You Don't Tug on Superman's Cape	60
The East Side Story	62
A Prayer for Las Vegas	64
It's Déjà vu all over again	66
Jerusalem	68
The Plot Thickens	70
A Year to Remember	72

Chapter Two
Year Two

Shameful	76
Deep State of The Union	78
Are You a U.S Citizen	80
Liberty Fading Fast	82

A Beautiful Mind	84
The New Dawn Has Come	86
Nuclear Waste Management	88
He's Our President	90
Assimilation	92
The Lost Inner Hippie	94
Why You Lost	96
The Korean Summit	98
Myth Busters	100
The PC Virus	102
Hypocrisy	104
Grasping for Straws	106
God Giveth, God Taketh	108
Schools Out Forever	110
Pittsburg	112
Let the Battle Begin	114
Melania	116
Out of the Shadows	118
Death of a Party	120
The Info War	122
Light After Dark	124
Aces and Eights	126

The Repress — 128
Constitutional Test — 130
The High Wire Act — 132
One Vote — 134

Chapter Three
Year Three

The Death of Criticism — 138
Shock of the 9th Circuit — 140
Oh General, Our General — 142
The Wall — 144
A Prayer for General Flynn — 146
Democrats Hopes and Dreams — 148
Don't Let the Door Hit You — 150
Grounded — 153
A Voice from Inside — 154
Not So Special Counsel — 156
Nightmare on Main Street — 158
Spending a life in Prism — 160
Tongue-Tied — 162

A Depraved New World	164
The National Compact	166
An Easter Call to Action	168
The Equality Act	170
The Republic in the Balance	172
Enemies Within	174
Independence Day in DC	176
Our Vision is 2020	178
The Death of America	180
The Wolf of Hollywood	182
Walking the Plank	184
The Debaters	186
They're Coming for Us	188
Biblical Times are Upon Us	190
Blind Sighted	192
The Trump Derangement War	194
A Year to Remember	196

Chapter Four
Year Four

The Caine Mutiny — 200

Liberal Hopes for Impeachment — 202

Mar-a-Lago Chess — 204

Quid Pro Quo — 206

Reflections of the Rally — 208

Running on Empty — 210

Resist with Fists — 212

The Last Laugh — 214

IG — 216

The Day the Democratic Party Died — 218

Light the Chanukah Candle — 220

When the Laughter Stops — 222

What Really Matters? — 224

The Iowa Caucus — 226

Three Days of Drivel — 228

Nancy Cries Foul — 230

Trump's State of the Union — 232

Grave New World — 234

Punching Out the Ticket	236
Someone Wake Up Joe	238
The World Vacation	240
Phone Home	242
No Caps and Gowns	244
Wearing a Badge of Dishonor	246
COVID-19	248
Germ Warfare	250
SOS SOS	252
Safety First	254
Live Free or Die	256
The Prophecy	258
Contact Tracers	260
Backlash is a Bitch	262
Save our Country	264
I Woke in 2020	266
Cancelling America	268
No Right to Bare Arms	270
What's in a Name?	272
The Black Widow	274
God Bless Humanity	276
Courting Justice	278
The Curse Of 2020	280

Chapter One

Year One

Election Night 2016

Blue States were fading
All over the map
Polls told the story
Cable stations react

They expected a landslide
From West to the East
Middle America voted
Now poised for a feast

Flip-flopping logic
It must be a trick
Recount all those ballots
They couldn't resist

Behold the election
Shocking with awe
Trump is victorious
The Left never foresaw

The Electoral college
Took them to school
Democracy preserved
Constitutionally cool

The First Term, Through Poetry

Hillary's fireworks
Became duds on the street
Democrats wailing
Finally tasting defeat

Campuses scramble
To find a safe space
Congress upheavals
All over the place

The die has been cast
Conservatives glee
Perhaps God intervened
So we dropped to our knee

So now time will tell
Our history's tale
We pray for our President
That peace will prevail

— *Written by RayRay*
11/9/16 ©

Irvin R. Brookstein

Ground Zero

It didn't take long
As they say
With tempers hot
On marching day

Grab your sign
Stating facts
Don't you love
Our pussy hats?

We don't care
If you agree
We won't get down
Upon our knee

We hate you Trump
We hate that voice
Can't wait to change
Electoral choice

Every minute
Of every day
Every hour
In every way

The First Term, Through Poetry

We'll kick some butt
In the street
Vomiting
Each time you tweet

Someone wake me
From my despair
Nightmarish visions
Of Orange hair

So just be ready
On the spot
We will hit you with
Our best Left shot

— *Written by RayRay*
1/22/17 ©

And the Ban Plays On

He put his foot down
Just like he had said
Some feel outright betrayal
When constitutionally read

Iran flexed its muscles
To no ones surprise
For within every action
Its opposite lies

Just like a tuning fork
Which resonates sound
Can only reach balance
When it slows itself down

He knew taking action
Would set off alarms
Awake from a slumber
Of significant times

So the Ban has begun
And protests abound
I noted no casualties
At least.. none could be found

— *Written by RayRay*
1/28/17 ©

ICBM

You may be a hawk
Or you may be a dove
But Iranian missiles
Are more than a shove

It's not wise to provoke
In aggressive detail
It's more than just testing
It's Peace that could fail

It didn't take long
For this man voted in
To put them on notice
Their thinking won't win

Peace is our purpose
But sometimes it takes
A fervent response
When our Freedom's at stake

It's never good timing
When dealing with this
Testing our mettle
But we have to resist

Perhaps economic
Diplomatically framed
But pushing the button
We have to restrain

So take a deep breathe
And softly exhale
Trust that our leadership
Heads will prevail

— *Written by RayRay*
2/1/17 ©

The Battle Begins

The sabers are sharpened
The lawyers are swift
Orally arguing
Whether borders exist

Some see the matter
As simple and sane
Can we choose who comes in
On the refugee train?

While no one disputes
The American dreams
Loving Lady Liberty
And all what that means

Our times are quite different
Real threats are abound
Do we abandon our sovereignty
Due to loudness of sound?

The lawyers will argue
The judges will test
Constitutional issues
Neutral from the protests

The First Term, Through Poetry

We voted them in
Appointed them too
Americans live by the outcome
In spite of our view

Some vowed they would leave us
Depends on who wins
I'm not sure that that happened
One-way tickets turned in

We live in a Country
Where diversity thrives
With Our One Constitution
Guiding our lives

So before we go crazy
For sanity's sake
Let the process unfold
Our Country's at stake

— *Written by RayRay*
2/6/17 ©

Once Upon a Time

Once there was tolerance
We gave each a chance
Now we'll bury an adversary
Because of their stance

Once there was Justice
Now just a rope
Guilt from a mob
While proof is a joke

Once there was Freedom
To say what you felt
Now watch your own back
And prepare for a welt

Once there was a Country
For me and for you
Now it's divided
Broken in two

Once there was pride
And bounce in our step
Now there is violence
From Right and the Left

Once we were Patriots
With similar thoughts
Now an internal battle
Is about to be fought

Once there was Brotherhood
Sisterhood too
Now we are Colorblind
It's either red or it's blue

Once there were symbols
Appealing for peace
Where has the love gone?
With hate on the increase

It's time to take stock
Give the process a chance
Change is uncomfortable
A new step in the dance

Believe in Democracy
It's not on the run
It's still solidly here
Good things still to come

Have a positive outlook
It works ever so well
It's time that our oceans
Have a more positive swell

— *Written by RayRay*
2/16/17 ©

The Press Conference

He didn't hold back
Not quite tactful redress
He poked and he prodded
And skewered the Press

While Bibi departed
And doing his job
He showed the prime minister
How to make shish kebob

He answered all questions
Some felt he abused
Not pleased that he mentioned
They were trolling fake news

The pundits reported
Chaos and dread
So he stepped to the podium
And condemned what they said

If you're looking for change
To the man at the mic
Then believe the tooth fairy
Will deliver your bike

We believe in Free Press
That's unquestionably true
For the voice of the people
Should always shine through

But you can take to the bank
How Press Conferences will go
When you deal with this President
It's all part of the show

       — *Written by RayRay*
       2/17/17 ©

The Roast

They invited him
But he won't go
Be in the crosshairs
To the flamer's throw

He faces fire
Everyday
He won't give in
To be their prey

They'll put a target
On his head
To make sure that
Their lion's fed

While most roasts
Are for comedy
Where you bite your tongue
And take the heat

This one comes
At such a time
Frankly it's his choice
To decline

The First Term, Through Poetry

These correspondents
May stomp and pout
That the one they sought
Has slithered out

But it's not so bad
I have no doubt
Let them enjoy
Their dinner out

But this time
The tradition bent
The sitting duck
Will not relent

So lick your chops
To your dismay
This time this one
Got away

— *Written by RayRay*
2/25/17 ©

Speech to Congress

As I watched
It dropped my jaw
Tears of Joy
Just drenched the floor

It's not like I hadn't
Heard before
Similar words
He would implore

This man takes it
On the chin
Impervious to pain
Poised to win

I hoped this time
He could captivate
Even those
Intent on hate

Mrs. Owens
Tore my heart
When she looked above
I fell apart

That one moment
Galvanized
A Country needing
That cleansing cry

The First Term, Through Poetry

Boldly speaking
From his Heart
Uniting us
For a brand new start

What struck me most
Through my tears
Was how far we've come
In 250 years

Last night marked
A brand new day
An American President
I'm proud to say

I believe in him
Though many laugh
I hoped he touched
The other half

— *Written by RayRay*
3/1/17 ©

Irvin R. Brookstein

Y R Taps

It's out in the light
How dark it's become
Where ever you turn
We're under a thumb

We should not be surprised
It's been going on years
From M to James Bond
And all of their peers

Internet companies
Cell carriers too
Even your TV
Is listening to you

There's no place to hide
Appalachia too
They're tracking your movements
To Moonshine and Brew

Every Americans
Very smart phone
Even a dumb one
Won't leave you alone

This is America
While it may be absurd
Whether we like it or not
They record every word

The First Term, Through Poetry

We hope they decipher
The good from the bad
The right from the wrong
The mad from the glad

So stay off of your phone
TV or PC
Get to the beach
Or a mountain top peak

Then whisper your message
Right into an ear
Out in the open
Where no one can hear

If that doesn't work
Then all we can say
Privacy's history
In the U S of A

— Written by RayRay
3/9/17 ©

Slip Sliding Away

It's slipping away
In front of our eyes
The end of Free Speech
So don't act so surprised

What have we wrought
Inside of our child
We thought tolerance lives
Instead it's gone wild

We thought American Campuses
Were places to learn
Explore ones future career
Not set fires to burn

We cannot sit idly
It's no time to hush
Put hands in our pockets
And say what's the rush

Don't wear your red hat
Don't show your true face
The wave that's forthcoming
No greater disgrace

The First Term, Through Poetry

Instead we take shelter
We're lying in wait
Better grab Constitutions
Before it's too late

The elders got wiser
While the youngins got dumb
We softened their instincts
They avoided our thumb

So now we behold
The Generation called Z
While the Boomers are vanishing
Like you and like me

What kind of legacy
What have we left
Just a slippery slope
And a freedomly theft

— Written by RayRay
4/27/17 ©

Sorrow in Manchester

When a child becomes a target
It's like a clever to our heart
How sick the mind to murder one
And be rewarded for their part

A future done forever
The light of someone's life
The darkness of the moment
Endless grief consuming strife

Our precious little treasures
Become our precious teens
Maturing into an adult
Await their family dreams

Their safety is our burden
We have to take a stand
Do whatever must be done
Because it's gotten out of hand

Our Children are the future
Every single one
Fighting existential threats
The time to act has come

Regardless of your party
It's not a time to blame
It's time we stand together
Let no parent face this pain

If it takes a bow and arrow
Or a sharpened bayonet
We have to fight them at their source
Because no other choice is left

— *Written by RayRay*
5/23/17 ©

Irvin R. Brookstein

American Pastime

What started with practice
To cover the base
Was shattered by gunfire
Such a bloody disgrace

Some said they deserved it
How callous and mean
Our Congressmen targeted
Is completely obscene

I lived through the madness
Of assassins crosshairs
Brothers Johnny and Robert
MLK and despair

I know there's desperation
When life has its pain
But to see Democracy's progress
Go completely insane

They wanted to savor
The green of the turf
Shag a few flys
And slide in the earth

The First Term, Through Poetry

Just live a life freely
Safely and rich
With bat, glove and baseballs
And whacking that pitch

It's time we remember
It's not for fortune nor fame
Just serving their country
And the love of the game

— *Written by RayRay*
6/21/17 ©

Irvin R. Brookstein

Patriot

It's hard to be a Patriot
And stand up for your flag
To put your hand upon your heart
When others think it's sad

It's hard to be a Patriot
To feel that unity
To know that call for freedom
To some a travesty

It's hard to be a Patriot
To know the love of home
To love that hallowed piece of ground
While others throw a stone

The causes will confuse us
So trust what's in your heart
The answer stretches everyone
When seams get pulled apart

The meaning of a Patriot
Will stand the test of time
Every human everywhere
Will struggle to define

The First Term, Through Poetry

So draw your own conclusion
Wrangle with the thought
It's time we all address the word
For the meaning we have sought

To call yourself a Patriot
Is not a dirty word
To believe it might be otherwise
Is clearly quite absurd

— *Written by RayRay*
7/4/17 ©

Baby Boomer Amends

It's been about 50 years
Since the offensive named TET
But the only offense
Was never honoring these Vets

We protested this war
One never declared
50,000 daughters and sons
Their deathly burden to bear

Be careful to criticize
Those whom dodged and deferred
Some forget it was commonplace
To hide in the herd

We mourned for the soldiers
Who never came back
Yet abandoned survivors
When they undid their pack

Some without limbs
Bodies abused
Chemically altered
Agent Orange infused

The Courageous came home
To a shameful disgrace
Some were offered a job
But most.. spat in the face

The First Term, Through Poetry

We worry more about climate
And fresh water to keep
Than finding a home
For a Vet on the street

These brothers of war
Continued the fight
Desert Storm Iraqi freedom
With no end in sight

Haunted by memories
Mentally and physically harmed
Suicide's rampant
Yet no one's alarmed

It's never too late
Helping those in despair
It takes more than a pill
Or a Psychiatrist's chair

Let's start with a hug
For love that was lost
Fix the VA
No matter the cost

It's time we pay homage
To the last of these men
And the irony of all
Is that they'd gladly do it again

— *Written by RayRay*
8/6/17 ©

Irvin R. Brookstein

Rewriting History

The World has gone mad
It's so simple to see
Because we don't like it
We will erase history?

Thinking they're cleansing
Rewrite it themselves
Might as well burn a book
Right there on the shelf

Reminds me of Adolph
Jews piled in a hole
Erasing their history
So truth can't be told

To those that repeat this
A lesson not learned
Pull down a monument
A confederate flag you will burn

The Washington monument
Demolition you'll see
Because tree huggers got angry
Because George cut a tree

But of course when it suits them
They'll connect their own dots
Compare Donald to Hitler
Whether truthful or not

The First Term, Through Poetry

Thinking this strategy
Will pay off in the end
But it's them that are fascist
Though they'd like to pretend

We may not be proud
Of deeds we have done
There's no one alive
Who hasn't done wrong

But burying history
Will not fool a soul
We pray we survive this
So our children will know

That history teaches us
The good and the bad
Let them judge for themselves
Not on some invisible pad

— *Written by RayRay*
9/1/17 ©

Disgrace and Offend

I know you're not offended
When they burn our US flag
But if they fly a confederate one
I suspect you'll be steaming mad

I doubt you'll be offended
When they behead and brutally stab
But you'll protect sanctuary criminals
In point of fact ..be glad

You're not at all offended
When they abort an unborn child
But you'll rebuild transgender bathrooms
So they urinate in style

You're clearly not offended
When they ambush sitting cops
But corralling gangs of felons
Makes you pissy poop and plotz

You proved you're not offended
When an obstructing congress stalls
But God forbid they fortify
A porous southern wall

The First Term, Through Poetry

It offended your left wing morals
When the electoral vote came down
Trump was elected president
Foiling Hillary Clinton's crown

So bring on 2020
When re-election day is through
So we can relish 4 more years
Of deplorables offending to you

— *Written by RayRay*
8/13/17 ©

Irvin R. Brookstein

Impeach This

So go right ahead
And give it a try
We're anxious to see
More Liberals cry

We saw the same tears
When Hillary caved
She slid down the tubes
Watched Democracy saved

So go right ahead
Knock yourself out
Spend precious time
Just flailing about

Every new day
You grow angry and tense
Dread seven more years
Of Donald and Pence

So go right ahead
And give it your all
Gather up your support
But prepare for the fall

You'll rely on amendments
And hope they will work
But it's gonna take more
Than naming a jerk

The First Term, Through Poetry

So go right ahead
And hire your best
Law firms with grudges
And hope they attest

Prepare for a battle
Like a snowflake in May
It will melt every time
No matter what you may pray

So go right ahead
Let the Congress impeach
It will collapse in the sand
Like the castle on the beach

It's time to face up
That impeachment's a fraud
Political science will fail
When experiments are flawed

— *Written by RayRay*
9/1/17 ©

Irvin R. Brookstein

Don't Tug On Superman's Cape ©

The climate is boiling
Hurricanes are destroying
The Congress is annoying
Let's blame it on Trump

North Korea's provoking
Marijuana's been toking
Emissions are choking
So Blame it on Trump

Woman are freaking
Abortions they're seeking
Fracking is leaking
It's gotta be Trump

Whites are depleted
Blacks are mistreated
Immigration impeded
It must be the Trump

Healthcare is fleeting
The Russians conceding
That Hillary's been cheating
The reason is Trump

The sun didn't shine
Poor grapes on the vine
While newspapers whine
It's all due to Trump

The First Term, Through Poetry

It must be his power
Leaping over Trump Tower
Clark Kent every hour
His Superman stunt

One man gets the credit
No one lets him forget it
That he wasn't vetted
The Nation's been stumped

So let's hit the piñata
Treat him as fodder
His sons and his daughter
Everyday they get dumped

So blame this one man
As much as you can
Just don't let them pass
A kryptonite Ban

— *Written by RayRay*
9/13/17 ©

Title credit to ©
Jim Croce ..RIP

Irvin R. Brookstein

The East Side Story

Up at the podium
As foe or as friend
He's on the East side
At the aging U N

They all sat dumbfounded
Not even a peep
In 30 odd languages
Translating his speech

All Heads of State
Headphones on their ears
Hearing him bury you
It just might appear

This man at the mic
Won't stop letting it go
No fear in his voice
Make sure that they know

The choices they make
He made it so clear
It's socialism they seek
Lands them flat on their rear

The First Term, Through Poetry

Who could have thunk it
Elton's words would forebode
Foresaw North Korea's dictator
A Rocket Man show

In front of all of those flags
So each country behold
Whether a Shark or a Jet
Len Bernstein's story's retold

— *Written by RayRay*
9/21/17 ©

Irvin R. Brookstein

A Prayer for Las Vegas

They came for a concert
They came there to play
The best Strip Show on Earth
Was Humanity on display

Hijacking trucks
To transport those hurt
Shielding your loved ones
Left your own blood in the dirt

Bullets reigned down
From a hotel in the sky
With no place to run
And no place to hide

Brave and courageous
Were EMT's and POLICE
Risking their lives
To get this sniper to cease

Nine minutes of terror
Bodies all lain
500 plus Americans
Left wounded or slain

We pray for their healing
We honor the dead
What happened in
Vegas is mourning instead

Coming to grips with
These hateful details
But I'm placing my money
That LOVE will prevail

Your Candlelight Vigil
Brought us to our knees
Graceful and caring
For times just like these

The debates will continue
Answers will be sought
But blaming and naming
Will add up to naught

Long Live Las Vegas
This City of Sin
You showed the whole world
That you know how to win

— Written by RayRay
10/4/17 ©

Irvin R. Brookstein

It's Deja Vu All Over Again ...Yogi Berra

They say that Trump colluded
To steal the votes away
The Russian bear intruded
Spoiling Hillary's glory day

The Cold War hasn't ended
It's heating up indeed
No different than the race to space
Perhaps Uranium increases speed

We paint them as the boogeymen
Just like on Halloween night
Wooden dolls are nesting
Must be the Trojan horse inside

Some curse the name of Putin
But on the other hand
We're making deals behind closed doors
Assisting Mother Russian Land

They helped us on the Eastern Front
Squeezing Hitler's frozen troops
But a Communist's a dirty word
That's what we learned in school

It is a world community
So Let's reach out with our hands
It's time to stop confusing us
About their insidious plans

I think of my descendants
Who grew up in the East
I still enjoy a Polish
Russian Vodka kielbasa feast

Please put aside hysteria
In spite of what is said
Red is still a primary color
Not a place to dread

— *Written by RayRay*
10/24/17 ©

Jerusalem

290 miles long
9 to 80 miles wide
The sea to the West
Enemies on all sides

Israel's sovereignty
Always put to the test
The World's eyes are upon them
A US Embassy move they detest

For 2000 years
The World would reject
Won't consider Jerusalem
A capital to respect

Who stands for Israel?
Raise up your hand
Built from the ashes
Of dry desert sand

Enter our President
So new on the job
Shaking up History
Making them sob

We committed to Congress
To move 60 miles East
But hid behind waivers
By past Presidents so weak

The First Term, Through Poetry

The World is alarmed
That peace is at risk
Move to a new building
They just couldn't resist

Their people rejoice
Let the opposition rage
I'm applauding our President
For turning the page

For 5000 years
The Jews got displaced
Holocaust in the 40s
I'm '48 given their space

So burn up those flags
Of Red White and Blue
But to the Israelis
This ain't anything new

— Written by RayRay
12/17/17 ©

The Plot Thickens

Agatha Christie
Is astir in her grave
Watching from Heaven
How politicians behave

Causing each side
Enduring distress
Wishing they had minicams
On the D.C. Orient Express

Peering inside
Of Mueller's war room
Laden with operatives
Putting Trump in their zoom

Discovering iPhones
With dubious texts
Demoting attorneys
God knows who will be next

Conspiracy theories
Who dunnits abound
No one trusts anyone
While Miss Marple's around

Confusing the Public
As to whom is to blame
Clues that confound us
May drive us insane

The First Term, Through Poetry

The Department of Justice
Plus the F B of I
Intelligence committees
All questioning why

One side determined
To bring down the King
While the other side hunkers
Their heels in the West Wing

It feels like a movie
In front of our eyes
With an ending I'm betting
Will be a clueless surprise

— *Written by RayRay*
12/8/17 ©

A Year To Remember

It's hard to believe
His first year has passed
Millions still abhorring
How the ballots were cast

Still shaking their heads
They still can't conceive
They're afraid to imagine
What lies up his sleeve

The pundits were stumped
While Hollywood wailed
Madonna's in Portugal
Her records have flailed

Gorsuch confirmed
Sessions was named
Mad dog promoted
Conservatives reign

NOKO is arming
Strutting their stuff
Sometimes you lose
When called on your bluff

The Eclipse casted a shadow
Harvey blew through
Puerto Rico got leveled
And they blame it on you

The First Term, Through Poetry

The Wall's still an issue
Tax code being reviewed
Healthcare is sickly
The Left feeling blue

Players are kneeling
Ignoring the flag
Hailing freedom of speech
Either way it's so sad

Antifa is ready
As Anonymous states
Leftist's scream towards the heavens
From a nightmare awake

What lies ahead
We can only surmise
But for many Americans
Tensions surely will rise

So it's on to year 2
Let's be hopeful at least
We pray that the Sun
Will still rise in the East

— *Written by RayRay*
11/8/17 ©

Chapter Two

Year Two

Irvin R. Brookstein

Shameful

They travelled to China
For a game in Shanghai
Entered Louis Vuitton
For sunglasses to try

Perhaps they didn't have money
Or their credit was low
Didn't convert Dollars to Yen?
So they did a shoplifting show

It doesn't take much
To make a mistake
Three lives in the balance
For the sake of a take

Thank god for our Leader
And President Xi
Diplomatic intervention
While in China agreed

The charges were avoided
They came home with their team
Safely back on the campus
Saved from a nightmarish dream

Suspended indefinitely
UCLA would detail
Better to sit out the season
Than ten years in a communist jail

They apologized profusely
But the best thing of all
We heard a presidential thank you
From these three Bruins so tall

So I shouldn't look past
Not a time to mince words
After a two year mountain of criticism
He got some credit he deserves

— Written by RayRay
11/15/17 ©

Irvin R. Brookstein

Deep State of the Union

The enemy works
In insidious ways
They used a fake dossier
To avoid wire tap delays

No one takes notice
It's a means to an end
Forget about legality
They won't have to defend

Judges were complicit
Attorney's were slick
The Department of Justice
Knew this was a trick

Hillary skated
From her illegal device
Comey's baloney
He never thought twice

One day we love him
The next day we abhor
He lays out a prosecution
She escapes thru the back door

The First Term, Through Poetry

Any ordinary American
Would be put behind bars
The charge would be treason
And that's just the start

Trump saw this was coming
They'd be after his hide
Always be aware of your enemies
From the inside

The Russian collusion
Diversion was fake
Distracted our attention
From an insidious deep state

Though he was duly elected
They sought to unseat this star
Shame you didn't recognize
This was a real coup d'etat

— *Written by RayRay*
1/27/18 ©

Irvin R. Brookstein

Are You a U.S Citizen?

The simplest of questions
Sets off fire alarms
Better not check the wrong box
And do yourself harm

Deep in your sanctuary
Keep taking the dole
While a hard working American
Knows the definition of stole

Why the objection?
To counting our heads
Unless your illegal
Then that question means dread

The Census has meaning
Every ten years
Determines representation
Make sure federal funding adheres

But the truth of the matter
Is that it hits a raw nerve
Pits a conservative agenda
That non-citizens don't think they deserve

The First Term, Through Poetry

Volumes of lawsuits
Will appear at the gate
Ludicrous and bigoted
Aren't arguable debate

This simple type question
Is loaded for bear
Let the Supreme Court determine
If this question is fair

— Written by RayRay
3/27/18 ©

Liberty Fading Fast

They're looking for dirt
Beneath any stone
Dastardly means
To dethrone the throne

Searching and seizing
With Gestapo like speed
Feasting on our liberties
Like piranha's who feed

Where are the Libertines
Who champion the cause
The ACLU will only
Stand silent and pause

A client and attorney
We're once protected from harm
Better learn signing language
Because that privilege is gone

No one is safe
From the arm of the law
When you insert Politics
It's worse than before

Our dear Founding Fathers
Astir in their grave
Their Bill of Rights fading
Seems that no one will save

The tipping point is upon us
The Law's out of hand
Witness the American Castle
Wash away with the sand

— *Written by RayRay*
4/10/18 ©

Irvin R. Brookstein

A Beautiful Mind

He hasn't yet completed
His first Presidential term
But already some textbooks
Make him appear like a worm

Shame on the school boards
For judging his brain
Indoctrinating children
Don't decry and defame

Their job is to teach them
How to write and to read
Adding some numbers
Learn technological speed

Have them think for themselves
Stand on their two feet
Not politically brainwash
Due to Hillary's defeat

Teach them the value
Of freedom of choice
Don't dictate your history
They should have their own voice

The First Term, Through Poetry

These children are precious
Our future in hand
Teach them about Civics
The Rule of Law in our land

Inserting your politics
Has no place in your school
Go preach to your own choir
Not inside of their room

Start with a prayer
Crossing their heart
Let them rejoice in our freedom
Which sets America apart

Give them pride in our country
Not divide them in kind
Polish don't tarnish
Their beautiful mind

— Written by RayRay
4/20/18 ©

Irvin R. Brookstein

The New Dawn Has Come

Awaken Awaken
From the shadow of doubt
The Left's freaking out
That you sense your way out

Awaken Awaken
The path is lit up
Like a runway at midnight
Though it may be bumpy and rough

Awaken Awaken
To the truth of our time
We know you are willing
To cross over the line

It's gonna take courage
To put on that hat
Make your America great
With a turn of your back

They've fed you a line
Bait sinker and all
They put crap in your head
Time to answer the call

The scale that you'll tilt
With the cast of a vote
Sending a message
For the World to behold

The voices of freedom
Always come with a cost
Indeed you've paid dearly
While hope never lost

So Awaken Awaken
You can't be denied
Our arms are wide open
Welcome to the Right side

— *Written by RayRay*
4/25/18 ©

Nuclear Waste Management

Their base is aghast
They'll refuse to admit
The depth of his actions
So decisive and swift

He's a fly in their face
A pain in their neck
At last someone defied them
While He'll never get their respect

He's aware of the danger
But up to the task
Iranian Nuclear Deal
Is over at last

They got pallets of franklins
They popped their champagne
Stirred up centrifuges
Now empty bottles remain

We'll get scorn from our enemies
While the Israelis rejoice
They're listening to tweets
Of our Conservative voice

Today he made History
We are ever so proud
To the Left's Global Order
One more piece taken down

— *Written by RayRay*
5/9/18 ©

Irvin R. Brookstein

He's Our President

It's not for his glory
Nor for fortune and fame
Only the jealous
Would sing that refrain

It's not for his ego
He's got plenty of that
He's willing to do battle
Take them down to the mat

He didn't lay fallow
Behind Country Club Walls
He followed his instincts
And answered our call

It's gonna take muscle
With elbows of grease
To wrestle with enemies
Intent on disturbing our peace

You may disagree with his manners
He's not Emily Post
We needed a fighter
Not a partying host

The First Term, Through Poetry

There are demons among us
Pledged to tear him apart
They've been secretly plotting
Right from the start

We have to support him
Do all that it takes
Help fend off his detractors
While our Country re-makes

Patriots love him
Especially his pace
He's our gift from the heavens
Shielded by all of God's Grace

— *Written by RayRay*
5/13/18 ©

Assimilation

When we entered the harbor
You could hear our refrain
God bless that we made it
We will honor her name

Just a dime in our pocket
And a hand cross our chest
Pulled a wheelless foot locker
Along a steerage like deck

Off to find work
Because there isn't a dole
Grateful to find space
In a tenement hole

Learning the language
With no quiz or test
Putting two words together
It was tough I confess

We didn't jump fences
Make demands on our hosts
We tried to fit in
And assimilate most

The First Term, Through Poetry

We kept our old culture
Especially the food
We shared it with neighbors
Lived the Goldenly rule

We raised up a family
We taught them about
The beauty of America
Is not a place to act out

We came in here legally
Enduring much pain
But the hope that they gave us
We would never defame

We welded we melded
We sweated and prayed
God Bless you America
Till the end of our days

— Written by RayRay
5/18/18 ©

Irvin R. Brookstein

The Lost Inner Hippie

It is difficult to imagine
The flip upon your switch
You once rallied for a peaceful world
But Trump's a negotiating bitch

You cheer for WAPO Bernstein
Applaud his Watergating fame
But when Trump uncovers Spygate
You spit spew and defame

You rose against oppression
Always came to its defense
But a vicious gang like murderer
You'll help across the fence

Your Be-In's for humanity
For the safety of a child
But You won't protect the dear unborn
Choose to fund PP's murderous ride

You cursed the FBI and CIA
When they bastardized your rights
Now you let them come right in
Allowing Gestapo raids to spike

The First Term, Through Poetry

You fought against corruption
Felt fairness had its place
Now care less of her bleaching bits
Nor dead balloting disgrace

It just confounds my sanity
That fifty years have passed
The beauty of that tie-dyed shirt
Has faded in the grass

— *Written by RayRay*
5/25/18 ©

Irvin R. Brookstein

Why You Lost

You're still scratching your head
Why y'all lost
Do you need calculators
To add up the cost?

You treated illegals like heros
And Citizens like trash
Gave the invaders the perks
For us a kick in the ass

You disrespected our flag
Claimed that God is a joke
Never thought for a minute
The fire you'd stoke

You marched for the women
While forgiving the rapes
Accepted Weinstein and Clinton
Democrats handed them skates

You funded Planned Parenthood
Sacrificed the Unborn
Peddled news that is fake
Ignored that you were forewarned

You attacked Christianity
Indoctrinated our young
Hate our Second Amendment
And the right to a gun

The First Term, Through Poetry

You labeled us racists
Won't consider a wall
Claim that we are all idiots
So we answered the call

There are so many more factors
That you'll never see
Because Liberalism has blinded
What it takes to be free

So we voted in places
That you'll never get
You see that there's plenty of space
Between East and the West

So behold the new landscape
With the Mid-terms at hand
We will surf that tsunami
And vote to reclaim our land

— *Written by RayRay*
6/3/18 ©

Irvin R. Brookstein

The Korean Summit

They'll soon land in Singapore
Both sides on the ground
I had to search google
As to where it is found

The Southern tip of Malaysia
Surrounded by Sea
Close to the Equator
Very humid and green

The Media's ready
They'll prepare for a spin
Can't let on one ounce
That we are poised for a win

It took sixty odd years
Now the table is set
To stabilize all Nations
From a Nuclear threat

We pause to honor the soldiers
A conflict forgotten in name
Finally at rest with the notion
That their efforts weren't in vain

Korea got split
Along a parallel line
Perhaps a goal of this Summit
Can erase it this time

Godspeed to our President
So committed to Peace
We pray for his Wisdom
So his wonders won't cease

— *Written by RayRay*
6/6/18 ©

Irvin R. Brookstein

Myth Busters

They said with the button
He couldn't be trusted
Yet with a peaceful Korea
That myth has been busted

They said with his temperament
He couldn't think clearly
But his newly imposed tariffs
May keep jobs needed so dearly

They say he's a charlatan
Corrupted and fake
Lowered taxes and border crossings
That's real for God sake

They say he's a misogynist
Casting women aside
Yet he hires the best of them
Who serve their Country with pride

He's absorbed every punch
Even Ali would be proud
Myths that he's weak at the knees
But you'll never knock this one down

Parading psychiatrists
About his tyrannical ways
Myths that he's Mental
And that we've been played

They perpetuate stories
They fabricate lies
Only dead air under their wings
So their myths never fly

— Written by RayRay
6/12/18 ©

Irvin R. Brookstein

The PC Virus

I've never understood
Politically correct
I thought communication
Should be something more direct

When you tippy toe around it
You hide the real effect
Shielding what you really mean
Will make it circumspect

It's gotten to the point
Because it's harder to detect
It's time we should reveal the truth
Which talking heads protect

So instead of talking straight
It's vagueness they elect
God forbid you tell someone
Their nonsense you reject

Offending is off limits
So feelings don't reflect
They anesthetize the issues
To truth that you inject

The First Term, Through Poetry

So lost in their delusion
So worried about their tact
While I'd prefer the bloody truth
Than lie to interact

When deception is your strategy
Of this I can be sure
The virus that's infected you
May never have a cure

— Written by RayRay
6/4/18 ©

Hypocrisy

It makes us go crazy
That they haven't a clue
When you knock on their noggin
But nothing gets through

You remind them of positions
They preached in the past
They only shrug shoulders
They hoped no one would ask

It must be amnesia
Leaves them in the dark
Even though audio and video
Confirms every remark

They figured their mouth
Always has two different sides
One convenient one not
So each day they decide

They toss out Integrity
Never seeing the loss
They hoped no one was watching
When they altered their course

A hypocrite never acknowledges
That perhaps they were wrong
So they turn it around
Sing the flip side of the song

They will never come clean
Their dishonesty complete
Their only motivation
Is retaining their seat

— *Written by RayRay*
6/15/18 ©

Irvin R. Brookstein

Gasping For Air

When your Vessel is SINKING
Because your portholes are LEAKING
Your bilge starts a FREAKING
Better grasp for the STRAWS

When your strategy's FAILING
And you thought you were SAILING
Your insults start WAILING
Better grasp for the STRAWS

When your rope starts UNRAVELING
On the road you've been TRAVELING
And your logic starts BABBLING
Better grasp for the STRAWS

When your platform is SHAKY
Your splintered news is all FAKEY
For God goodness SAKEY
You've been grasping at STRAWS

When your speed's getting SLOW
And there's no place to GO
And your HIGH ROAD became LOW
Now you're grasping at STRAWS

When your Party just STALLS
You start climbing the WALLS
You fumble juggling BALLS
Better grasp for your STRAWS

When your head feels the THUMP
And your throat feels the LUMP
It's the MAGIC OF TRUMP
He just snipped all your STRAWS

— Written by RayRay
6/18/18 ©

God Giveth God Taketh

We ache to the core
It tears at our heart
Your loved one leaves for their job
And fate rips life apart

We never know why
We never know when
A kiss good bye in the morning
Yet never see them again

It could be at a movie
At the school down the street
At a club going dancing
Or just walking the beat

When facing pure evil
And there's no place to run
The last line of defense
May be someone's hand on a gun

There won't be a protest
Kids on a Capitol Hill train
Just the grief of the loved ones
For only their ashes remain

Forgive all your loved ones
No matter the cause
We see that life is so fragile
We have to take pause

God giveth God taketh
Not much more we can say
Just drop to our knees
And be grateful today

— *Written by RayRay*
6/29/18 ©

Schools Out Forever

I can't say I blame them
For protesting guns
They took hold of an issue
Because before there was none

The Left so misguided
There issues inane
Pass on to these children
Infused in their brain

Forgetting Scalise
Ignoring poor Kate
Car attack in NY
Chicagoland fate

Pressure from peers
You cannot object
Your bully type pulpit
Constitution you'll wreck

Classes abandoned
Teachers behold
Political protest
On the School District's dole

Building an army
Of misguided youth
Democratic voting block
While hiding the truth

The First Term, Through Poetry

Suppressing free speech
Abortion's disclaimed
Won't walk out of your classroom
While those issues remain

You're blaming the weapon
Instead of the man
A new law on the books
Wouldn't save one life at his hand

We must protect students
Inside of their schools
Posting trained and arm guards
Just like the Israelis must do

It's not about guns
Or laws you can change
It's more about morals
And Illness of brains

— Written by RayRay
3/21/18 ©

Irvin R. Brookstein

Pittsburgh

My raw thoughts are circling
Around in my head
Where is the outrage
That another eleven are dead?

Instead, point middle fingers
That our Leader's to blame
We can't wear a Hat, Star or Cross
Hate of the Sabbath is given no name

Your silence is deafening
Revealing the truth
You're not contrite in the murders
Must believe it's righteous to do

Democrat hopefuls
Muslim leaders en masse
Avoid condemning the carnage
Figure votes will give them the pass

Those with a heart
Are grief stricken today
Yet the haters could care less
In fact, prefer it this way

It's chilling to see this
The death of your Souls
So consumed in your hatred
Morality and judgement just froze

This same sickening mantra
Death to the Jews
If not by gas or an oven
Then bullets right in the pews

We must take a stand
We know what to do
Keep those complicit, from power
God gave us this moment to choose

— *Written by RayRay*
10/27/18 ©

Irvin R. Brookstein

Let the Battle Begin

So the people have spoken
The ballots are in
Many are happy
But others chagrin

The price of our Freedom
Is the shift in the winds
Flip flops are inevitable
Another cycle begins

The House has been taken
The Democrats elate
The Senate more reddened
Hunkered down to their fate

The President's still standing
As he prepares for a fight
Is that Impeachment on the Horizon
The House flexing their might

Is his Agenda in jeopardy
What will become of our gun
Will we be building The Wall
Will ICE melt in the Sun

The First Term, Through Poetry

All sort of questions
Will come into play
He seeded the Court
Perhaps Trumping the fray

The future's always uncertain
It's rather complex
So onward to 2020
The Presidential election's up next

— *Written by RayRay*
11/7/18 ©

Irvin R. Brookstein

Melania

The way she's been treated
Is nothing short of obscene
She's been a breath of fresh air
Rarified, classic and clean

Swept away in a torrent
Of political gain
Yet she's a rainbow that glistens
After a blistering rain

Never gracing a cover
Of one magazine
It clearly broadcasts a message
How they're so ragged and mean

Her grace is unmatched
Her mothering true
Raising a prince
Until the battle is through

She's a beacon of beauty
A modeling gem
With womanly facets
The Left won't ever defend

The First Term, Through Poetry

She stands by her husband
Through thick and through thin
She's fluent in language
Yet so soft spoken within

She's caught in a history
Which she didn't choose
She's a shining example
In spite of the abuse

God Bless our First Lady
God speed as you go
Millions adore you Melania
We just thought you should know

— *Written by RayRay*
10/23/18 ©

Irvin R. Brookstein

Out Of The Shadows

The strength of our Leader
Is a miracle indeed
Even the largest of Countries
Have been brought to their knees

They've abused us on trade
And poured through our gates
Responsible for our fallen
Including Bombs they still make

We are clearly more respected
On the World Stage
Previous leaders did falter
Were weakened and caved

But the real raging battle
Is right here on our shores
Corporations that feel
They're an untouchable force

The Hallmark of Freedom
Is our ability to speak
Sharing our message
Without thought blocking police

If you're platform is Public
Then the ideas need to be
Out from the Shadows
And politically free

The First Term, Through Poetry

We hope that our Leader
Takes them to task
These censorship programs
Must be unmasked

The greatest collusion
Is shielding the light
Attempting to blind us
When we're in a fight

These powerful platforms
Must answer the call
Just like other Countries
Insuring what's better for all

— *Written by RayRay*
7/26/18 ©

Irvin R. Brookstein

Death of A Party

From when I was young
By twenty-one and a half
I always voted for Democrats
Or my peers they would laugh

We never debated it
As far as I knew
That was the party
From the people's point of view

JFK was my hero
I remember the day
I was a boy in 5th grade
In downtown Dallas fell prey

McGovern and Muskie
Carter and Bill
Barry out of Nowhere
Then the Hillary pill

Something terrible's happened
They're lost in a maze
Someone Kidnapped the Party
Tragic..like a Shakespearean play

I feel so ashamed
At the way that they act
The Party I loved
Now there's no turning back

I could never imagine
It frazzled my mind
To think that a citizen
Is now last on the line

They want to hijack our country
And give it away
Brainwash our children
Our flags we cannot display

We're at the fork in the road
One way's a dead end
Time to take the RIGHT turn
Until our last breath we'll defend

— *Written by RayRay*
7/31/18 ©

Irvin R. Brookstein

The INFO WAR

They're banning our tweets
Surveilling our texts
I would not be surprised
If the Bible is next

It's an all out assault
On our freedom of speech
Drawn from the playbook
That the Communists teach

In the Late Thirties
In a Germanic pile
The lit up the textbooks
And let suppression run wild

Controlling the message
So the people are blind
So only the tyrants
Get to brainwash the mind

Let me be perfectly clear
About this freedomly theft
It comes not from the RIGHT
But from the activist LEFT

When you corner an animal
By asserting your might
Be prepared for a facelift
From the claws in the fight

It's about our Nations survival
The Jews say it best
NEVER AGAIN
With a passive protest

We pray that our Leader
Recognizes the risk
So the Country we're fighting for
Will forever exist

— *Written by RayRay*
8/6/18 ©

Irvin R. Brookstein

Light After Dark

There are forces among us
With a dastardly plan
They wish to open our borders
While they take the gun from our hand

Pundits predicting
He will fall on his face
Congress obstructing
When he puts plans into place

The Media's mocking
This bird everyday
The Bashing of Faith
Just won't go away

Our Allies complaining
And sometimes resist
The guard that is changing
Who wrestles their wrist

Our enemies are watching
To see if we fail
They see our divisions
In bristling detail

The opposition party
Wants to undo
Whatever we stand for
In their radical view

The First Term, Through Poetry

But we are the people
We voted him in
We stand here United
We will never cave in

We will not let the voices
Stifle our cause
This Political crisis
Puts our head in their jaws

History is upon us
We've seen this before
We can never allow Freedom
To exit our shore

So dig in Dear Countrymen
Throughout this beautiful land
The result we are seeking
Sits in the palm of our hand

— Written by RayRay
8/19/18 ©

Irvin R. Brookstein

Aces and Eights

I'm so tired of collusion
That's starts with an R
For over two years now
They've played the Soviet card

They dealt us a hand
So that we'd be played
The Media Mavericks
Blessed the charade

But the deck has revealed
That the cards had been marked
It was American Collusion
Right from the start

Barry was phoning
About things he would change
So the Uranium One deal
Wouldn't go up in flames

Strzok and his minions
And other sharks in the moat
Revealed their intentions
To choke our President's throat

The First Term, Through Poetry

She paid for a dossier
Salacious in scope
Bluffing the Country
Pinning their hope

They shuffled the FISA Court
To approve wiretaps
Framed conversations
But we smelled a rat

Then in comes Mueller
Who arrives on his broom
Acting like Hoyle
With his own set of constitutional rules

So they've set up the deck
Holding it close to their vest
But our Eyes In The Sky
See a scam at its best

— *Written by RayRay*
8/9/18 ©

Irvin R. Brookstein

The Repress

When I look through the paper
All that I see
Is a constant bombardment
Of President T

It could be in Boston
New York or LA
Go put down your Dollar
And see what they say

It's all been prepared
From a single digital file
One common story
Politically vile

Gone is the concept
Of reporting the news
When they secretly join forces
So they can skew and abuse

They were given the right
Number One on the Bill
But not to become
One political shill

Your deceiving the people
By coloring the feed
You've violated our trust
And let Fascism breed

But we won't be fooled
We hold the key to your locks
Thank God what is still sacred
Is the balloted box

— Written by RayRay
8/12/18 ©

Irvin R. Brookstein

Constitutional Tests

Let's put into perspective
Just what's supremely at stake
For a few generations
The court can remake

The Left wants this Body
To be their own political troll
Squeezing our Country
Like a square through a hole

The Right on the other hand
Is not trying to bend
We simply ask that they follow
What our Constitution intends

Executive Privilege
Should remain on the slate
The Electoral system
Not be up for debate

The right to a Vote
Must be in a Citizen's hand
Not to those who jump fences
And expect to demand

Our Freedom of Speech
Must always remain
Colluding to shadownban
Has gotten off of the chain

The First Term, Through Poetry

Our right to protection
Must not be undone
Whether a Sovereign Border
Or possessing a gun

Every American
Has got to come first
Including the pre-born
Stop public funding a curse

These fundamental issues
Hang on their scale
Pray they be blinded to politics
Let inalienable Justice prevail

Life Liberty and Happiness
Is what our Founding Fathers foresaw
Not to be molded by power
From the Congressional Floor

— *Written by RayRay*
9/4/18 ©

Irvin R. Brookstein

The High Wire Act

Oh my God another clue
Anonymously leaked
In jest to wear a wire
Gives us ample pause to think

Graham Bell and G Marconi
Invent a wireless technique
Another link upon the chain
Collusion on the brink

It starts to fit together
Of course they will deny
The bias in the echelons
A twenty-fifth Amendment try

It appears we need a dentist
To deal with this decay
When abscess gets into the bone
It's time to take the teeth away

Thank goodness that our President
Is always steps ahead
He'll be cautious not to fire them
And let them use their rope instead

The Left will claim it's tyranny
When the tumblers start to count
Let God reveal the truth to us
Like Two Tablets On the Mount

— *Written by RayRay*
9/22/18 ©

A Vote

You're only one person
It may seem you're alone
You may ask does it matter
That perhaps you'll stay home

The Earth keeps on spinning
The Sun dawns in the East
The Tide's high or its low
There's no sign of the beast

Life can deceive us
We become blind to the plot
You may not feel hot water
Till you're boiled in the pot

The Forces of Evil
We have seen on display
The core of our Freedom
Could quickly slip slide away

Don't let complacency fool you
You still have your power in hand
Press down on that lever
Our last hope to demand

The First Term, Through Poetry

God gave us the power
Joining your hand in mine
A deluge of water
Starts with one drip at a time

One single vote
We've seen its power retard
Spoiled the crown on her head
When we drew the Trump Card

So grab onto your neighbor
Read them this poem
A single vote can bring victory
Thus preserving our home

— *Written by RayRay*
10/3/18 ©

Chapter Three

Year Three

Irvin R. Brookstein

The Death of Criticism

It seems more than ever
That criticism is dead
Now it depends on your color
What's allowed to be said

Be careful of gender
Religion or Race
Don't dare comment on ideology
Or you'll become a disgrace

Whether it's warranted
To call someone out
For their illicit behavior
Or the hate speech that they spout

The rules of confronting
Have dramatically changed
It's seems now that only White skin
You're allowed to degrade

Don't make a black person a target
Don't take a Muslim to task
Don't call a Woman a liar
Suggest removal of an antifa mask

The First Term, Through Poetry

But if you're a Caucasian
A Judeo-Christian or Male
If you believe in two genders
It's you they'll assail

These criticisms are allowed
Everyone else gets a free pass
They can say what they like
Never pay when they sass or harass

It brings me no joy
That I should have to insist
For the illusion of White privilege
Earns me a welt on my wrist

— *Written by RayRay*
11/13/18 ©

Irvin R. Brookstein

Shock of the 9th Circuit

Call in the electrician
911 on your phone
You're in for a shock
The 9th Circuit is blown

Its wires got crossed
Come as fast as you can
It's the same faulty circuit
Blown during a traveling ban

The President is hot
Because the breaker got thrown
Seems the AC to DC
They shut off on their own

The area affected
Includes nine Western States
Plus two Pacific Islands
Perhaps their billing is late?

The power's shut off
Can't close up the gate
The caravan seeks asylum
No time for a Border debate

The Supreme Court is watching
These current events
Leave the 9th Circuit alone
Justice Roberts for their defense

Will the decision hold water?
There's an 80% chance
In spite of the sparks
The high court reverses their stance

So put on your galoshes
When a wire is down
To fix the 9th Circuit
Will take more than a ground

— *Written by RayRay*
11/24/18 ©

Irvin R. Brookstein

Oh General, Our General

The unbridled joy we are feeling
We can barely contain
God rewarded our efforts
A brilliant rainbow after the rain

That grain of injustice
So irritated our core
Single minded our purpose
We dug in like never before

Heartened yet sorrowed
Your life and family at risk
So many years in the making
They act like it didn't exist

Serving our Country
In Peace and in War
He became his dutiful counsel
In the midst of a storm

A probe with the purpose
Of unseating our man
He got caught in a crossfire
That he hadn't planned

But the strength of our General
Goes above all the rest
How he reacts to adversity
When he's put to the test

He looked out over his troops
With tears became overcome
Grateful, so thankful
For what his supporters had done

So General our General
We've got your back
With Faith Family and Friends
You'll be back on the track

— *Written by RayRay*
12/5/18 ©

Irvin R. Brookstein

The Wall

The Wall is not a concept
Nor a symbol to insult
The Wall is not a theory
Nor an algebraic note

The Wall is not a statement
Nor an answer to defend
The Wall is not a vision
Of what the Right wing doth intend

The Wall is not a figment
Of an imaginary brain
The Wall is not to crucify
For legal Immigration will remain

So let's say exactly what it is
And make it very clear
A Wall to but a barrier
Between countries that are near

The Wall is there to demarcate
The Border loud and clear
It's to prevent those intent
On illegally coming here

The First Term, Through Poetry

A Wall is made of metal
Or a Brick and mortar smear
The Wall is built in such a way
That sneakers won't adhere

The Wall protects our sovereignty
Each Nation has this right
We don't care if your offended
Nor if the height will cause you fright

It's time our Nation took a stand
And fund this needed Wall
But different than the "Field of Dreams"
For they won't come at all

— *Written by RayRay*
12/11/18 ©

Irvin R. Brookstein

The Eve Has Come

You stand at the precipice
Don't ever give in
You know that the heart of a lion
Knows only to win

You were born for this moment
Trained by the best
You executed strategy
Catapulted past all of the rest

You know what to do
Hold your head high
Have Faith that the Lord
Will see through Sullivan's eye

Take a deep breathe
Let go and let God
Restore your dear family
And have evil retard

Joyous in knowing
That this day will be
Redemptive and glowing
Blissful and free

So many behind you
Some you can't ever repay
It's Love that will find you
Make this a most beautiful day

— *Written by RayRay*
12/17/18 ©

Democrat Hopes and Dreams

In just a few days
The House Reps. will flip
We'll do tumbles and cartwheels
Champagne we will sip

We're hiring lawyers
From all over the map
We care not how you do it
Make him tap-out on his back

We want to view Tax Returns
Oh please let us see
The illicit contributions
On schedule A, B and E

We're waiting for Mueller
To target that Man
Bring us collusion conclusions
As fast as you can

Show us his financials
From Moscow to Prague
Penthouse apartments
List the bunnies he flogged

Allow Sanctuary Cities
To thrive in the burbs
We pray for the recovery
Of Ruth Bader Ginsburg

The First Term, Through Poetry

We hope the "Me Too" movement
Protects every last tribe
Except for the Jews
Nor anyone on a Conservative side

Give every illegal
Who wants to come in
A voter registration
Let the harvesting begin

Please ignore the problem
Of Drugs and Human Trafficking Et al.
Nix every proposal
For building a Wall

These are our wishes
For Twenty Nineteen
We're not asking for much
If you know what I mean

— Written by RayRay
12/29/18 ©

Don't Let the Door Hit You

I started scratching my head
As to what Ocasio did say
Take away everyone's wealth
So we are all paupers that way

This is the definition of Communism
As Karl Marx would relay
The Government controls everything
A Russian and Chinese forte

So where's the Collusion
With Russia today?
It's not with Trump nor the Deplorables
You see..We won't give it away

So the real Russian colluders
Are the people who say
Let's open the borders
Vote ..then take their money away

So One Half of the Country
Is really to blame
Renaming Democracy
Swapped it for a Communist name

The First Term, Through Poetry

If this is what you want
We will offer to pay
Pack up your Bags
And do not delay

Head West past California
Wave to Hawaii below
You can thank Ms Mayzie bird
For the sh-t show she spoke

Go directly to China
Or to Moscow in tow
In fact sneak over the Borders
And let us know how that goes

— *Written by RayRay*
1/7/18 ©

Grounded

To The State of the Union
She demands a delay
So he makes a quick move
By grounding the plane

You think you can wrestle
With the Commander in Chief
Better unpack your bag
To your own disbelief

You think you wield power
Hold the Congress purse strings
But forgot it's the American people
Who pay for these things

Air Force One is symbolic
Of American might
Just like the Sovereignty of our Border
War heroes died for that right

So before you book travel
On An American dole
First Take care of our Business
By Fulfilling your Leadership role

— *Written by RayRay*
1/17/19 ©

A Voice From Inside

A flutter a heartbeat
A life underway
A tiny kick from inside
I'll be welcomed one day

I hear your voice echo
In my tiniest ears
You're singing a song
It even tingles my rear

Tho I haven't discovered
What's happening to me
Yet I feel every vibration
Of my own history

One day I will tell you
How grateful I swear
I am the miracle
Not a burden to bear

I hear there is trouble
So cruel and absurd
Adults who grew hardened
Would slay me I've heard

How did this happen?
Such murderous lies
If it's a sin on the outside
What's the difference inside?

The First Term, Through Poetry

Someone please tell me
It's really insane
Conception has happened
Yet I am to blame?

Someone please shield me
From those who don't comprehend
That the smallest among us
Are those we must always defend

I'm the human in humanity
That starts with one cell
Let me breathe some fresh air
I promise a great story to tell

— Written by RayRay
1/25/19 ©

Irvin R. Brookstein

The "Not So" Special Counsel

The Fox is in the Hen House
They should have never let him in
He's devouring the Patriots
His mission masks a sin

A Shark is in the Fish Tank
Preying for a meal
Anyone within his path
Is at risk and that's for real

A Bull is in the China Shop
He shattering the glass
The Constitution made it clear
But this one's got a pass

We see where this is going
Foolish we are not
You claim that you seek justice
But frankly it's a crock

It's time we see the documents
Let the Americans decide
Not crouch behind redacted text
To cover what you hide

The Balance in our Government
Resides among the Three
How can a Special Counsel
Usurp the founders plea?

If impeachment is his purpose
Let our Leader pull the plug
It may land before Nine Justices
Let them see beneath the rug

As far as I can tell
He's under the D O J
That's within the Executive Branch
So why not fire him today?

It's time we fought the fire
That's raging wild and free
He plans to burn down Patriots
It's awfully plain to see

— *Written by RayRay*
1/27/19 ©

Nightmare on Main Street

I could swear it was real
There was sweat on my brow
It jolted me out of my sleep
We've lost it somehow

A troubling nightmare
No more American flags
Statues all lifted
Right down to their pads

Walmart was shuttered
So were the malls
People all wearing
Head coverings and shawls

No more white picket fences
Can't smell baked apple pies
No more churches with steeples
With people inside

Banks with some names
I could not recognize
Globalist something
Are we even surprised?

The First Term, Through Poetry

Clinics and Doctors
Advertising with pride
Arrow pointing shingles
This way to infanticide

The best of America
Had been hung out to dry
Nothing is left
But the salt track of a tear from my eye

— *Written by RayRay*
1/30/19 ©

Irvin R. Brookstein

Spending a Life in Prism

This rainbow of colors
Has me twisted in two
We identify people and causes
By the shading of hue

I can not understand
Why Green gets to be clean
Thus dissing the Irish
If you know what I mean

The Color of Yellow
Though the Asians object
Poor Banana Republics
That get no respect

The Color of Purple
Was a movie I knew
Now it identifies States
Who combine Reddish and Blue

Black was for Power
What's become of their stork
More babies are aborted
Than born in New York

I used to love Red
Gorgeous Dresses and Shoes
Now hats signal imminent danger
And cause Russian collusion abuse

What's happened to Orange
Is clearly obscene
They've packed it with Calcium
So it's no longer so sweet

Alas there is White
No longer a Lily at all
It's become quite a target
Their privilege I just can't recall

It's time we abandon
Using labels so cruel
Just let live and let live
Like a box of crayons in school

— Written by RayRay
2/5/19 ©

Irvin R. Brookstein

Tongue-Tied

The Framers knew the risk
Of a voice that's loud and free
First Tyrants aim to cut your tongue
Then tie your hands and feet

They'll make you the example
Right in the Village Square
Expose the sacrificial lamb
So others wouldn't dare

But the Hallmark of our Freedom
Was etched in number One
Freedom to express ourselves
Must never be undone

We see attempts to stifle us
Each and everyday
Giants of the Media
A deadly game they play

We aren't part of Asia
Nor in the Middle East
You've never seen resistance
Just try and steal our peace

The First Term, Through Poetry

To those of you who lead the charge
You're held in high regard
Please know that we all have your back
Our oppressors we'll retard

It's time that we respect the words
That The Founders carved in stone
While they came not down a mountain
They wanted it to hang upon our home

— *Written by RayRay*
2/10/19 ©

Irvin R. Brookstein

A Depraved New World

They're coming for our guns
They're coming for our steak
They're out for every dollar
Only Vegans can partake

Biology is history
No more She and He
An Hermaphroditic Nightmare
As far as eyes can see

They've stifled all our voices
They're listening on our phones
Installed their nasty webcams
In the bedrooms of our homes

They're kicking down our doors
In the middle of the night
They're teaching every child in school
That only traitors put up a fight

They'll legislate morality
According to their code
Slippery sleazy stealthy thieves
A New World Order we are told

Free speech has expired
You'd better toe the line
God and Bibles off the shelves
Judeo-Christians left behind

The First Term, Through Poetry

Obedience demanded
Slavery's back in place
Four-Hundred years of Freedom
Gone without a trace

If you think this can not happen
You'd better think again
The Wolves were voted into Congress
That Sheep can not defend

We had better poise for battle
Because Freedom is at risk
Paul Revere reminding us
The real meaning of resist

— *Written by RayRay*
2/15/19 ©

Irvin R. Brookstein

The National Compact

There is clearly subversion
Behind every move
Like unseating our Leader
Who is deep in a groove

Now The Electoral College
Is under attack
States passing Amendments
Which put a knife to our back

It's slick and it's stealthy
A legal assault
Back to a popular vote
To Lock up their vault

Their goal is quite clear
270's the prize
They will take down our Republic
In the blink of an eye

California and New York
Would determine our fate
Kiss representation goodbye
For many a State

Steering elections
For decades to come
Radical leftist progressives
Put us Conservatives under their thumb

Slowly and sneaky
Imperceptibly Sly
Putting Lex Luther in charge
Before any asked why

We better wake from our slumber
And plan our defense
Fight legal Fire with Fire
Directly.. without any pretense

This is our last stand
To defend what we must
Saving America
Or risk reducing it....to dust

— *Written by RayRay*
4/16/19 ©

Irvin R. Brookstein

An Easter Call to Action

Antisemitism is rampant
Congresswomen unload
Churches are burning
All over the Globe

The Pope's mostly been silent
Behind Vatican walls
Attacking on Easter
In front of us all

The Media's complicit
Obscuring the news
Political Correctness
Only disguises the Truth

It's time for confronting
The root of the cause
These Jihadi terrorists
Are usurping God's Law

We've allowed this to fester
We've put our heads in the sand
What is urgently needed
Remove the sword from their hand

The First Term, Through Poetry

Every Synagogue and Chapel
Must sound the alarm
Fight Fire with Fire
Until the Enemy is gone

All Christians and Jews
Must answer the call
Uniting as allies
For once and for all

This Globalist agenda
Will spell our demise
But Just like the Savior
It's time we arise

— Written by RayRay
4/21/19 ©

The Equality Act

I woke up this morning
And decided to be
The girl of my dreams
Fancy and Free

So I tucked in my privates
Put a scarf on my neck
Went to the mirror
For one final check

Today I'm a female
I can go where I choose
Are there stalls in the bathroom
Or do the urinals I use?

Off to the workplace
Perhaps H R will allow
A change of my gender
Will my income equality endow?

Called my life Insurance Agent
Female costs will suffice
After all, Now I'll live longer
Fool the actuarial charts and the price

The First Term, Through Poetry

I've upset the Adamly Apple cart
Flipped humanness on its head
Let's throw out all of the text books
Make a transgender edition instead

I can't wait till tomorrow
Continue this new gender attack
It's weird, I feel manly
It's indeed an equality act

— *Written by RayRay*
5/18/19 ©

Irvin R. Brookstein

The Republic in the Balance

It feels like the calm
Ahead of the storm
Declassifying the plot
And how it was born

Deep Stately Operatives
At the top of the heap
Must be held accountable
For the Coup they did reap

Let the truth be exposed
Once and for all
History needs to behold
How close we came to a fall

A President elected
The People had spoken
Yet Puppets and their Masters
Attempted to revoke him

We gave them the power
To spy and surveil
Enemies of our Country
Not for political blackmail

We must teach our children
The lesson at hand
A crystal clear view
So they will understand

That Freedom is precious
Forged from our past
The blood of the fallen
So a Republic would last

The chapter on tyranny
Must be written alas
Not allowing the traitors
To be given a pass

So take a deep breath
Drop down to your knee
God has not forsaken
Our Inalienable right to be Free

— Written by RayRay
5/29/19 ©

Enemies Within

They would have us believe
That there's threats on the globe
Fake News about Russians
Purposeful distractions have gotten quite old

The threats from Iran
And the value of Yen
Xi and the Rocket man
Front pages they'll spend

But the truth of the matter
Lo and behold
The true threat to our Republic
Must always be told

Look no further than Congress
And to the endless fake news
Letter Agency seditions
Spying and FISA abuse

Stealth from the wealthy
Pulling strings with a stench
Unfriendly circuit court orders
Right from the Bench

Pelosi and Soros
Schumer and Schiff
Keep pushing us closer
To the edge of a cliff

The First Term, Through Poetry

Jump over the Border
Tunnels under the fence
Give them voter ID's
Let the elections commence

Ilan and Rashida
Who will they defend?
Won't take an oath on the Bible
The Quran is their friend

The Death blows to our Country
Here's the place to begin
The real culprits among us
Are the enemies within

— Written by RayRay
6/21/19 ©

Irvin R. Brookstein

Independence Day in DC

We came from all corners
Of Cities and States
Our purpose was Patriotism
We know Freedom's at Stake

We Raised our Flynn Banner
Defending our Man
Books that were written
Displayed on a stand

We toasted to friendship
Enjoyed DC till dawn
Harry's till closing
Sang our American song

We Huddled near Lincoln
In the drizzling rain
Breathtaking flyovers
To our President's refrain

Cementing new Friendships
In a House and Hotel
We hugged and we kissed
What else.. I can't tell

Boundless our Energy
Showing the way
Doing good for our Country
To our opposition's dismay

For we are Americans
We answered the call
Deeply believe in the meaning
Of Justice for All

For One special Holiday
Great Memories were made
Can't wait till next year
Perhaps an Annual Brigade

— Written by RayRay
7/7/19 ©

Our Vision is 2020

They dread to hear the Oath
Our twenty twenty throng
They can't take that we'll celebrate
Another Inauguration song

To think that we'll have borders
Will drive them up a wall
That we'll uphold the rule of law
Well that's the best of all

It irks them that illegals
Will have to get in line
Behind those waiting patiently
While their shrinks work overtime

Our Vision is so joyous
They shudder at the thought
Of Congress back into the Red
Safe spaces will be sought

Suppression's in recession
Twitter lost the fight
Google lost their bugle
Searches finally Right

The First Term, Through Poetry

They hate that jobs are filling
That Wall Street's on a tear
Paychecks have more dollars
While Antifa doesn't dare

Their ballad of collusion
Hit the lowest note
All the Deep State players
Are seen jumping from the boat

I know it's just a vision
But it's no opticians joke
I can clearly view the opposites
If we should lose the vote

— Written by RayRay
7/13/19 ©

Irvin R. Brookstein

The Death of America

When the last statue is down
Pulled way down to the ground
And no more marble is found
It's the Death of America

When He and She's gone
It won't take very long
"They" will have no way to spawn
It's the Death of America

When they muffle our voice
And it's a crime to rejoice
We gave up our Freedom of Choice
It's the Death of America

When you can't genuflect
There's no Bible left to protect
God's given no more respect
It's the Death of America

When there's no School left to teach
Only what World Government's preach
Every child's out of our reach
It's the Death of America

When there's no Husband or Wife
They squeeze out all unborn life
The Family will never revive
It's the Death of America

When I can't write a verse
Recording this curse
It can not get any worse
It's the Death of America

When the last Battle is fought
And all hope has been lost
We watched knowing the cost
We never stood up for America

— *Written by RayRay*
7/28/19 ©

Irvin R. Brookstein

The Wolf of Hollywood

Another sad story
If It wasn't a spoof
Jussie Smollett
Is the Boy who cried wolf

Look at the rope
That circled my neck
Two large assailants
Two MAGA suspects

Attacking my gayness
Threw me off of my feet
Tho I didn't anticipate filming
From web cams on the street

It sounds like Tawana
And the Blazes of Ford
Uncorroborated stories
Ne're a truth to their word

But the damage is done
A Hypocritical view
Two types of Justice
For him and for you

This clever vignette
Designed to insist
But will the Grand Jury
Indict or slap on his wrist

His career will go on
Media protecting their own
Another slick trick agenda
To remove Trump from his home

But we always see through this
We'll never be fooled
We will strike back on the ballot
Yup.. another "Empire" schooled

— *Written by RayRay*
2/21/19 ©

Walking the Plank

They don't have a platform
Their planks are shaky and loose
The Green Deal is unholy
It lies and disguises the truth

Never a solid suggestion
They're mostly short on detail
Ignoring who gets the invoice
Then promise your check's in the mail

They want open borders
So only illegals prevail
While our Vets remain homeless
Wish to send ICE agents to jail

They've tried every last trick
In their Marxist playbook
They're the purveyors of doom
They could even sweet talk a crook

They're getting so desperate
We can smell their disgust
That aroma called "Fear"
Bottled as Democrat musk

They hope the Economy
Falls flat on its face
They care more for obstruction
To spite the nose on their face

They would shred every last value
Strip it down to its core
They could care less about Country
From the hills to the shore

But we are it's Patriots
We have our Forefathers to thank
Let's help them on with their blindfolds
And guide them right off the Plank

— Written by RayRay
8/20/19 ©

Irvin R. Brookstein

The Debaters

They took to the stage
To a round of applause
The Democrat hopefuls
Pleading their cause

Taking their turns
Bashing Trump and Old Joe
An Obama era leftover
From his head to his toe

Then there's unlikable Bernie
His face blotchy and red
You rubbed next to some static
Said the hair on his head

Kamala Harris
Never changing her clothes
Sarcastic bombastic
Only anger she shows

Elizabeth Warren
Still sings her charade
While Booker and Beto
Insist on a gun grabbing raid

The First Term, Through Poetry

Castro the disastro
His popularity is down
Even blessed Latinos
Would best run from this clown

Lizard tongue Pete
Anyone trusting his word?
Yang keeps us begging
For Ten C-notes on the 3rd

Finally there's Amy
Rational she seems
Appealing for Unity
Well Good luck with these freaks

— *Written by RayRay*
9/14/19 ©

Irvin R. Brookstein

They're Coming for Us

I can hardly get the words out
While I hear a piercing sound
The wake-up alarm is blasting
Yet there's snoring all around

The threat is clear and urgent
They've been banging on our door
Eviction notes are posted
Patriots sleeping on the floor

Three years ago we put him there
Each day fighting off a coup
Be clear the target of impeachment
Lands right back on me and you

Every value in our soul
Every fiber of our heart
Every ounce of fight within us
Must commit to do our part

Elected leaders sold us out
To their feeding frenzy yen
Year four forebodes a battle
That may never come again

For if they succeed in removing him
You can kiss our rights goodbye
They'll confiscate our Freedom
While we sat and wondered why?

We'll no longer wear a bright Red hat
The color Orange they have slain
Blue lives no longer matter
Green Progress...their refrain

So wake up every Countryman
Every Countrywoman too
Our way of life is under siege
The World must also heed the view

— *Written by RayRay*
9/30/19 ©

Irvin R. Brookstein

Biblical Times are Upon Us

Like David and Goliath
We're fighting for our life
They're Squeezing out the air we breathe
Censoring our rights

The middle ground exists no more
You're either for him or you're not
The Media won't tell us the truth
Lies are all they've got

Our Leadership is useless
They've abandoned ship
We the people are alone
Bailing out each drip

The odds are stacked against us
Persecution dawn till dusk
Grab your sack of sticks and stones
Our Survival is a must

We are taking fire
Patriots attacked
We used to be the honored class
Now they'll stab us in the back

We voted in the President
We put him in our House
They bugged the walls around him
His family and his spouse

We see there is no justice
No traitor dressed in chains
Sedition is their moniker
Till no Patriot remains

So keep your Bible in your pocket
Your hands upon your gun
Only when Goliath falls
May we claim the battle's won

— *Written by RayRay*
10/2/19 ©

Irvin R. Brookstein

Blind Sighted

I never thought "Whiteness"
Would fall on its face
How I was born
Would become a disgrace?

Hearing those that apologize
Makes me gag in my throat
Is this the same Country
Where Mother arrived in a Boat?

I've always been colorblind
To all that I see
Took pride that my conscience
Allowed others to be

Whether we talk of Divinity
Or Darwin's evolutionary tree
We come from the same root
Brothers and Sisters are we

What purpose does it serve
To Blame my White Skin
MLK talked mainly of character
Now it's "Gone with the Wind"[TM]?

The First Term, Through Poetry

This is dangerous territory
It could let violence take hold
Those that would attack us
Could multiply ten-fold

This smells just like Nazism
How they blamed all the Jews
For the sins of the World
Now it's come to skin tone and hues

I won't allow despicable Racism
To determine my fate
Best we fully expose this insanity
Before it's too late

— *Written by RayRay*
8/10/19 ©

Irvin R. Brookstein

The Trump Derangement War

The evil sharks are circling
Us supporters are the bait
We have to bring our own harpoons
Resistance can not wait

If you think that they'll take prisoners
You better think again
Their mantra of destroying us
Not if..but only when

Trump is but a symbol
Of everything they hate
Patriots are in the way
Of their socialistic fate

Congressmen and women
Haven't stood their ground
The Constitution's under siege
Yet only cowards can be found

So gather up our Veterans
Bring the bikers too
Hillbillies from the Hollows
The Storm's about to brew

So just in case you're wondering
What will he do next
He's donning boots with spurs and points
To do what he does best

He's Preparing for the Battle
Lawyers fighting for his life
Our Republic's in the balance
It is we who'll pay the price

So now we must support him
More than ever done before
This is no time to be civil
We're in a Trump Derangement War

— Written by RayRay
10/10/19 ©

Irvin R. Brookstein

A Year To Remember

It started with elections
Dems would take the House
They rubbed their palms together
Now we'll finally get him out

They pinned their hopes on Mueller
They want Presidential doom
So perplexed by his confusion
Sucked the air out from the room

He couldn't prove collusion
Obstruction's out the door
The Attorney General followed him
Spelled Spying for the floor

Next in came the Socialists
Who want to take our cars
No more trips on Aeroplanes
Nor cows upon our farms

Illegals storm the borders
Inner cities pay the price
Years of Liberal leadership
Account for their demise

Ten hopefuls took the stage
Waved goodbye to Bill of Rights
Plans that tax us close to death
Should they win Election night

Keep your gun inside your holster
Be sure to Pray to God each day
Raise your voice there is no choice
There's not a moment to delay

So Influence your neighbors
In spite of all the strife
2020 is around the bend
To retain our way of life

— *Written by RayRay*
10/1/19 ©

Chapter Four

Year Four

The Caine Mutiny ™

There's a Mutiny on the Bounty
Four Rats command the ship
Blackbeard Nan Pelosi
Nadler, Schumer, Schiff

They've swashbuckled the process
Every step along the way
To hell with any Rule of Law
They're Pirates seeking prey

It started on Election Day
Every minute they persist
They've boiled the blood of Patriots
We hate it's come to this

Our Republic teeters on the brink
The Left blinded to the truth
They've been sold a bill of goods
Their own Freedom they could lose

The Senate must reclaim the Deck
Bring the ball and chains
Traitors all must walk the plank
Till no Coup D'Etat remains

We're sick of flimsy evidence
There's no meat upon the rack
After three years of hoax and false arrests
It's time to take our vessel back

So you keep poking at the bear
Grizzly Black or Brown
Francis Key would clearly see
Our Flag will not be taken down

Don't let sedition derail our Chief
It's no time to stand at ease
It time our Armada point the guns
And take back the Seven Seas

— Written by RayRay
10/31/19 ©

Liberal Hopes for Impeachment

We've been crossing our fingers
Our eyes and our toes
We hate him with passion
We know that it shows

We've calculated the odds
Hedged our Liberal bets
We pray for one shining moment
On which we hope to collect

We're giddy, yet cautious
Can't be contained nor composed
Will we finally get him?
Remove the emperor's clothes

To heck with the evidence
Third hand rumor's enough
We believe that he's guilty
Watch as the Media sticks to its bluff

We will limit your questions
Prevent witnesses that may appear
We prefer Basement style Justice
Bounce him out on his rear

Be it treason or bribery
Or high crimes that we seek
Let's treat him like Kavanaugh
To dispose of this freak

To tell you the truth
It's not only about him
We want to stick it to you
Avert another Deplorable win

So Let the inquiry begin
In front of the lens
It's our hope for impeachment
Yes..we are at it again

— *Written by RayRay*
11/12/19 ©

Mar-a-Lago Chess

The Ambassador chessboard
Sits on top of his desk
It's up to him to determine
When a pawn's laid to rest

Most Americans relate to
How At-Will employment may go
Even though Marie was removed
Her direct deposits still flow

Ukraine's been an issue
About resources and political gain
A gas company paid money
Which Biden's son would retain

I find it amusing
That their case to Impeach
Is based on facts not established
On his phones calls and tweets

The chess game was started
By the previous king
But the Queen's failed Coronation
Spoiled the whole bloody thing

The First Term, Through Poetry

So all the corruption
Had to be redefined
Deflected towards Trump
To shield their own political bind

The House Castling will fail
While the Senate awaits
Setting up their own chessboard
With Hunter and Whistleblow dates

So the weekend's upon us
To give us a break
With both sides burning the oil
For next week's chess moves they'll make

— Written by RayRay
11/15/19 ©

Irvin R. Brookstein

"Quid Pro Quo"

This dubious phrase
Has been all over the news
Born out of Latin
For the World to confuse

It's been twisted and sifted
Since the beginning of time
I will scratch yours
If you will scratch mine

Now matter the meaning
It's a this for a that
Or if you prefer
A tit for a tat

Before there was money
I think you'd agree
If I give you something
It ain't gonna be free

The essence of barter
Is a trade that is fair
Both people are happy
With each that they share

It could be munitions
For a runway or base
It's not the size of the trade
Just that there's fairness in place

Granted there's issues
When politics is infused
Consider Lobbyist intentions
Which can get seriously abused

So Impeachment's before us
Quid Pro Quo they'll define
Thousands of years of its usage
Doesn't automatically make it a crime

— *Written by RayRay*
11/21/19 ©

Irvin R. Brookstein

Reflections of a Rally

They hate what's in our Heart
Incensed that we believe
That Freedom is the reason
They simply can't conceive

They shudder at the thought
When we gather in a hall
They wish that we would vanish
When we come one and all

They hallow in their misery
They want to eliminate the words
Christmas and Thanksgiving
And that we're feasting on the birds

Just look upon the crowd
See the smiles upon the face
We demonstrate that family
Has no gender, age or race

We're honor Life and Liberty
Pound our patriotic chest
Wear hats and pins and shirts
What we treasure, they detest

The Charlatans they worship
Would stomp us to the ground
Extinguish every ounce of breath
Suppressing every sound

It's our MIGHT they'll never muffle
It's our RISK they'll never take
While we BASK in GOD and GLORY
They prefer the dark and fake

That's why we RALLY for our Leader
AMAZED by what he's done
We're ENERGIZED by his belief
That the best IS yet to come

— Written by RayRay
11/27/19 ©

Running on Empty

You SAY that he's your nightmare
But he's our dream come true
You insist that he's a racist
You must be talking about you

You WISH you could invalidate
The votes which we had cast
Usurp our First Amendment
But suppression's out of gas

You HOPE to end his tenure
And throw him out the door
He'll order up his moving van
But not till after twenty-twenty-four

You HEARD there was collusion
With Justice round the bend
You forgot a lack of evidence
Is not needed to defend

You PRAY for his removal
But God has put him there
Your debaters haven't left the gate
Ten losing horses in despair

The First Term, Through Poetry

You MOCK the Constitution
Its meaning you would rob
The Founders clearly warned us
About a seditious future mob

You INSIST that you know better
By taking cars and trucks away
If you try to confiscate our guns
I'd be careful everyday

You FORGOT that we're united
Watch out when we are pissed
You've yet to see the worst of us
When our Freedoms are at risk

— *Written by RayRay*
11/13/19 ©

Irvin R. Brookstein

Resist with Fists

If you think they will befriend us
You'd better think again
Their goal is to destroy us
It's not an if, but when

If you should raise a question
They don't want you to ask
Their eyes pop out right from their head
Because you've taken them to task

Once they sense your color's Red
They mobilize their mob
Tho Turley voted Democrat
They did their death threat job

They'll intimidate the weakened
They strong-armed A T T
To release some private phone logs
Schiff undid their privacy

They threaten corporate business
Those mergers that we know
Warren wants to take them out
So that swamp can run the show

They'll tax us to oblivion
Suppress speech and what we think
Their fake Impeachment witch hunt
Puts our Freedom on the brink

It's time we clench our naked fists
Show them we will not comply
Those who wish to crush our votes
Will feel it right between the eye

So let's gather up dear Patriots
The battle is at hand
If we ever bow to tyrants
Kiss goodbye our Promised Land

— *Written by RayRay*
12/6/19 ©

The Last Laugh

We see the pressure's mounting
Their twisted tale's a joke
There's desperation on their face
Impeachment's up in smoke

They argued until midnight
Just what the IG said
Convinced there was no bias
So they put a mark upon his head

They know the clock is ticking
The election's close at hand
Deplorables are lining up
One huge rally'cross the land

This is why they must act quickly
Get deliberation's done
The Articles of Impeachment
To remove our Native Son

Their sadness, disingenuous
Their solemness, a lie
Their heavy heart's baloney
It's a good ole acting try

The First Term, Through Poetry

We see right through their strategy
They'll take the votes out from our hand
They never learned four years ago
We will protect our blessed land

So you keep peddling stories
As polls will sink to record lows
The only way to resuscitate
Is censure or let it go

Either way, get used to it
In the White House he'll remain
Five more year of Liberal tears
While laughter's our refrain

— Written by RayRay
12/12/19 ©

IG

All of us wonder
What the IG will say
We've waited four years
To our Judicial dismay

They've let devious players
Have the freedom to walk
Many granted immunity
So they won't have to talk

While many Trump allies
Got trapped in their web
They spied on insiders
So a Dossier could be fed

So who verified it?
Appears no one can say
If those FISA's were crooked
By God someone must pay

We're tired of hoaxes
Chocked full of lies
Reeking from leaking
In our nose and our eyes

The First Term, Through Poetry

We sit in the balance
Of our Republic's demise
If they reward this malfeasance
Kiss our Country goodbye

So watch for the spinning
No pinning of blame
It's been a four year faux story
Since down the elevator he came

I've said this before
And I'll say this again
If he survives till November
That's the only Justice my friend

— *Written by RayRay*
12/8/19 ©

Irvin R. Brookstein

The Day the Democrat Party Died

You can take it to the bank
You can chisel it in stone
You can mark this day of infamy
For it's theirs and theirs alone

They concluded in the House
On flimsy here-say they relied
Two Articles of Impeachment
But it's the Day the Party Died

Some are elated here in Washington
Democrat Leaders who complied
Schiff, Nadler and Pelosi
Will rue The Day The Party Died

So do they send it to the Senate?
Their case they just might hide
God forbid he gets acquitted
Reminded of The Day the Party Died

When the road you're on's dead ended
With no exit and no pride
They did these deeds based on a hoax
They caused The Day the Party Died

The First Term, Through Poetry

Better head back towards their drawing board
Barr and Durham will prove they lied
These reports will lead to torts
Justice for The Day the Party Died

Sixty years ago teenagers froze
Teardrops they could not hide
Rock n Roll collapsed they say
The day their music Died

Democrats must face the Music
And dirty players who contrived
Don McClean please sing again
About Buddy and the Day the Party Died

— *Written by RayRay*
12/19/19 ©

Irvin R. Brookstein

Light the Chanukah Candles

You may argue about the methods
Debating what's at risk
But there is nothing more important
Then their Freedom to exist

Persecuted in every Country
Their Temples they'll destroy
But enough Oil to Burn the Candles
For Eight days of Light and Joy

The Modern Jew is torn in two
What movement to believe
Historically they are Democrats
But it's Republicans who won't deceive

Nadler, Schiff and Schumer
Jews who answered the Congress call
Would not travel to Jerusalem
When the embassy moved its wall

Blumenthal and Bloomberg
Running on the Left
Mocking Trump and Kavanaugh
They're Jews who won't protect

Soros funding movements
Anti-Semitism on the rise
Born a Jewish Hungarian
Appears aimed at their demise

It's irks me to my Jewish soul
That I feel a sense of shame
So many prominent in Politics
But besmirching our good name

So tonight please light a candle
No matter what persuasion you may be
For if the Jews go down the tubes
They'll be no Freedom left for thee

— *Written by RayRay*
12/22/19 ©

Irvin R. Brookstein

When the Laughter Stops

For years they have been laughing
But today they felt the smack
Recollecting loaded pallets
Cold Cash to scratch their back

They chant Death to America
They kill our native sons
Their reign of terror never ends
Centrifuges they have spun

But they never could imagine
A Commander such as Trump
This Chief will pull the Trigger
He's a Rocket up their Rump

The media is spinning it
In Un-Patriotic style
Siding with the Terrorists?
They're so pitiful and vile

Red-lines are being painted
No more holding back
So brazen at our embassy
But they never expected this attack

The First Term, Through Poetry

He's redefining Leadership
He's making them think twice
He's put the World on notice
His response will be precise

While Schiff and Pelosi scramble
Again they're taking aim
That he didn't consult with Congress
Fodder for another impeachment claim

Gone is Al-Baghdadi
Soleimani, auf weidersehen
I no longer hear hyenas
No more laughter, only pain

— *Written by RayRay*
1/3/20 ©

Irvin R. Brookstein

What Really Matters?

It matters not, he took a shot
It matters not, about the fact
It matters not, a killer's down
They will never pat his back

It matters not, he speaks the truth
It will all be called a lie
These hypocrites deceiving us
Everyday as it goes by

It matters not, he has our back
Abroad or here at home
This man walks down a lonely road
Past a Congress cold as stone

It matters not, of what they say
It's all vinegar and salt
Thank god he speaks direct to us
Not through fake media by default

In spite of caustic words they write
They're called Pundits for god's sake
We know which traitors pay them off
They're just puppets on the take

The First Term, Through Poetry

They call us imbecilic fools
We're the mofos they detest
Smelly stupid ghastly ghouls
Our morals they reject

How they glorify these terrorists
Our Allies quick to reprimand
Slap his wrist while they resist
Until they need our helping hand

Let it be told that we won't fold
We will always answer to the call
It's only him and us and God we trust
That matters most of all

— *Written by RayRay*
1/5/20 ©

Irvin R. Brookstein

The Iowa Caucus

There is no shame in admitting it
That we are far from being in the know
What happens out in Iowa
May stay beneath a drift of snow

The Caucus is around the bend
An Iowan Field of Dreams™
Their thirst for wealth and power
The end justifying all their means

Sanders wants to lead the charge
Youth recalling they've been played
They still hope free will come to be
And not pee on their parade

Biden hopes to win the race
But he stutters at the gate
He just can't seem to connect two words
Will dementia seal his fate?

Warren spins some tales within
The Grim Reaper everyday
She thinks that she is Robin Hood
But it's the middle class that she would slay

The First Term, Through Poetry

Buttigieg thinks he's got the edge
Alfred E. Newman's his namesake
On the surface he sounds plausible
But underneath he's Mad-ly fake

Klobuchar has come quite far
With a "middle" point of view
But some would say, when you peel away
She's a Socialist through and through

Trump's impeachment calls from DC Halls
Keeps the Senators off the Trail
I can hear them groan and bitch and moan
They fear that both are bound to fail

— *Written by RayRay*
1/21/20 ©

Irvin R. Brookstein

Three Days of Drivel

It's gonna be epic
When they suffer the blow
When they crash to the ground
And there's no place to go

How deep their devotion
They believe their own press
Not even a whiff of a notion
That their propaganda hovers near death

They repeated a story
Through yawns and loud snores
Tiny widgets and fidgets
Could be seen from the floor

Finally resting their arguments
To a round of applause
Only not by the Democrats
But by Republicans who had to endure

Now the table is turned
Time to put this nonsense to bed
We may hear from a witness
Watch it spell doom and more dread

The First Term, Through Poetry

We Deplorables are ready
Saturday ratings will soar
Squelching their arguments
Into the Senatorial floor

For years they've been plotting
Now it's come down to this
We've waited our turn
Trusted God for this moment of bliss

It high time they tasted
Another crushing defeat
Seeing their crocodile tears
Splashing down to their feet

— *Written by RayRay*
1/25/20 ©

Irvin R. Brookstein

Nancy Cries Foul

Every pitcher knows the feeling
When the skipper walks the mound
It's time you hit the showers
Because your shellacking has been sound

The Speaker's become unraveled
Wild pitches West to East
So oblivious to signals
That a win was out of reach

The Media will surround her
Ask her what went wrong
Let's listen for excuses
She'll sing the same old song

The Verdict of Acquittal
She simply won't accept
No different than four years ago
When libs and snowflakes wept

She was basking in her glory
Ink filled her golden quill
One should never count one's chickens
When you're up against the People's Will

One wonders whether she'll survive
Stay third position from the top
Her secret dream to become the Queen
A perfect game became a flop

So back to San Francisco
Open up that Golden Gate
Better hang up your Stilettos
Your Hall of Fame will have to wait

      — *Written by RayRay*
      1/31/20 ©

Irvin R. Brookstein

Trump's State of the Union

Tonight he came out swinging
Left no prisoner in his path
A chance to vent, not to repent
Every word revealed his wrath

For three years he's walked a tight rope
The one they wished around his neck
Our base rejoiced, how he voiced
The values we respect

He blasted all the Socialists
Sanctuary cities came clearly into view
How he's eliminated terrorists
Decked the Obama White House too

Proclaiming each accomplishment
Blue collar dollars in the bank
The Last Tuskegee Airmen
Rush Limbaugh he would thank

He went for every jugular
Hit them right between the eyes
Watched them shrivel in rotunda seats
Those White suits mortified with sighs

The First Term, Through Poetry

He didn't talk of unity
Or bridging party woes
Because it wouldn't matter what he says
We know where all that goes

This was no time for mending fences
With his acquittal the next day
How awkward was this moment?
Eclipsed anything he could say

This night we be remembered
Filled with so many melancholy tears
Can't wait for each installment
Five more Trump State of the Union years

— *Written by RayRay*
2/5/20 ©

Irvin R. Brookstein

Grave New World

When you look upon the Stage
It becomes clearer what we see
The Yellow light's been flashing
To caution you and me

Look beneath these people
Below their practiced speech
Try measuring their true intent
It's vicious Government overreach

All I see is danger
It's not that far away
They'll be coming for our Liberty
On that cool November day

Kiss good bye the Constitution
Big cities rule the roost
Once they confiscate our guns
We'll have submitted to their noose

Taxes are perverted
We the People pay for free
The unborn may never take a breath
Uncle Sam brought to his knee

The First Term, Through Poetry

Wind turbines on our sacred soil
Electric Outlets on the street
Our kids become automatons
School indoctrination makes them weak

The Supreme Court is in shambles
Globalists take their seats
America has been sold out
The transformation is complete

So welcome to the Grave New World
If Socialists win the day
All those years of Blood, Sweat and Tears
We must not give it away

— Written by RayRay
2/21/20 ©

Irvin R. Brookstein

Punching Out the Ticket

We know there's speculation
Wondering who each pick will be
Will they wait for the Convention
Before Selecting their V P

Biden hopes to utter clearly
A clear as it can be
He can't remember diddly squat
But might remember his V P

Those Dubious Damsels in Distress
The ones who left the race
Identity Politics on the slate
These females squarely in our face

They're pitching their positions
They're only one heartbeat away
Worse than ten goldiggers
Because money and power are in play

Sanders he meanders
Don't know who his pick would be
He'd lean towards a Socialist
I see Liz upon her knee

Kamala with her animus
Amy acting sweet
Heaven knows Old Creepy Joe
May have visions of them off their feet

But the Nightmare of the Century
You know of whom I speak
She slithers just past justice
Plays Criminal hide and seek

Beating her was glorious
Repeating would be the same
Deplorable Elephants Don't forget
That Hillary is her name

— *Written by RayRay*
3/9/20 ©

Irvin R. Brookstein

Someone Wake Up Joe

Another day he's late
Tho he's got somewhere to go
Did someone mark the date
It's time to wake up Joe

Air Force One is waiting
The President's much too slow
The Pilot's contemplating
Where the heck is Joe?

President Xi is fuming
And Congress wants to know
Perhaps the tariffs are resuming
Could someone wake up Joe?

The Global temperature is warming
Oil pricing to and fro
The polar bears are yawning
We have to wake up Joe

The Cabinet is leaking
Their jobs could come and go
They're afraid of even speaking
Please someone wake up Joe

The First Term, Through Poetry

The Economy is tanking
Wall Street's gonna blow
It's Soros they'll be thanking
Should we even bother Joe?

The Globalists are laughing
Puppet strings they won't let go
New World Order increases Staffing
We won't need to prop up Joe

The Vice-President has been pacing
The 25th Amendment's set to go
The Power Play's ripe for the taking
Don't bother waking Joe

— Written by RayRay
3/10/20 ©

The World Vacation

The NBA is stuffing it
March Madness obsolete
The NHL's been put on ice
Cruise lines docking their whole fleet

Sanitizer disappeared
Toilet paper's off the shelf
Shopping Malls are empty walls
A Sunday Pastor by himself

College classes are remote
Spring Break has hit the brakes
Stadiums are empty bowls
FaceTime's doing double takes

No happy hours at the bar
Employees off the clocks
Socializing is taboo
Fist jabs are more like blocks

The President is taking heat
Though this is nothing new
Congress funded needed bucks
To see this crisis through

The First Term, Through Poetry

They call it a pandemic
It's a very scary sound
Microbes looking for a host
Contagions all around

We must protect the elderly
It's best they stay at home
Reschedule their appointments
They won't mind that they're alone

Let's focus on logistics
Perhaps we all can shut it down
We could use a three week World vacation
Till corona runs aground

— *Written by RayRay*
3/12/20 ©

Irvin R. Brookstein

Phone Home™

It woke me up abruptly
Could it be a dream?
Praise from Andrew Cuomo
Ilhan Omar on a helpful beam

Dana Bash of CNN
Praising Forty-Five
Did someone stick a pin in them
Is the MainSteam Media Alive?

It came upon us suddenly
As Epiphanies often do
We are all aboard One Worldly Boat
We're the Passengers and the Crew

We can't go to the movies
Airline travel is a bust
You're lucky if you can work at home
Online banking is a must

There's no time for Dirty Politics
When people need a helping hand
Time to focus our priorities
Cash, Food and Shelter in our land

The First Term, Through Poetry

It's times like these, in crisis
When fear can grip us all
We need information free of flaws
Leadership and healthcare are on call

I'm reminded of 9-11
When The Towers hit the ground
It was in that horrific moment
That togetherness could be found

So take a breath from panic
Dial a friend or family on the phone
Make sure that they are safe and sound
Because it's hard to stay home alone

— Written by RayRay
3/19/20 ©

Irvin R. Brookstein

No Caps and Gowns

Who could ever have imagined
That your Graduation Day
The day that you've been working towards
Got axed next month in May

Every field that's been endeavored
Every level that's been reached
That day to show the World you know
Got halted with a screech

No proms or commencement speeches
Nor Grandparents bearing gifts
No barbecues with hotdogs
Who would believe it's come to this

In my lifetime I can't fathom
This has never come to pass
A World has stopped right in its tracks
God knows how long it's gonna last

So take solace all you Graduates
One day you'll celebrate
You'll wear that Badge of Honor
Twenty-Twenty was your fate

The First Term, Through Poetry

Every Graduate you encounter
Will have that sadness in their heart
But the Bond you've shared together
Can not be torn apart

For me it's Fifty years
Since I wore my Cap and Gown
The year was Nineteen Seventy
Thank God I'm still around

So I tip my hat to everyone
Congratulations, just the same
Though commencement may have eluded you
Your accomplishments remain

— Written by RayRay
4/1/20 ©

Irvin R. Brookstein

Wearing a Badge of Dishonor

When this crisis is over
Just what will it cost?
Besides souls lost to the virus
Millions of jobs have been lost

This financial debacle
Might not be undone
To those small boarded up business's
When will their stimulus come?

They predicted that hospitals
Would be filled to the gills
If that's not what has happened
We've been had by a cabal of shills

But the real pending danger
Is a cold shift in the wind
A long list of Government mandates
Which are about to begin

Demanding compliance
Puts us under their thumb
Vaccinating our Nation
But at the point of a gun

The First Term, Through Poetry

They'll be inserting a cocktail
Deep into our veins
Remarkably, while no one protested
It left our Liberty in chains

Forget school for your children
No job there for you
Better display your "Medical ID" card
Just like the "Star" of a Holocaust Jew

You'll no longer have choices
You'll have to do what they say
The dream about Freedom in America
Became a viral nightmare today

— *Written by RayRay*
4/9/20 ©

Irvin R. Brookstein

COVID-19

No matter what your ailment
You can put your mind as ease
Your stroke's not gonna kill you
It's COVID-19 if you please

Your tumor's of no consequence
It could increase or it could shrink
But the logistics of statistics
It's COVID-19 what they think

If Your Heart Attack is minor
So that your blood clot doesn't show
Don't worry they won't check the box
It's COVID-19 as you know

The Flu ain't gonna kill ya
If you're snifflin or you sneeze
Put aside the box of Kleenex
COVID-19's the disease

No more natural causes
Our dear old seniors feel at peace
When we lay them down beneath the ground
Here lays a COVID-19 dear deceased

To Those Souls who are addicted
Or our Blessed Homeless on the street
If they succumb they'll add the sum
To the COVID-19 Sheet

If your A 1 C is tanking
And your sugar ain't so sweet
You can put aside your insulin
It's COVID-19 you couldn't beat

So morbidity doesn't matter
In spite of any cause
This is how they keep us down
With COVID-19 counting Laws

— *Written by RayRay*
4/18/20 ©

Irvin R. Brookstein

Germ Warfare

I am a microbe
You may try to defend
But it's me who'll be standing
When you come to your end

No matter your virtue
Whatever your cause
The material things that you've worked for
At death will be lost

I've been plotting against you
Since the beginning of time
But in spite of my game plan
You thrive and you shine

Although every last human
Returns to the Earth
Every year that you're living
You prove your value and worth

Ashes to Ashes
To Dust, as it's said
But you pass on your genomes
To those you have bred

You even have taught me
About the battle details
While death is to the body
I see that your spirit prevails

I've tried to detour you
The State wants to keep you in place
While we may look like bedfellows
A breath of fresh air feels good to your face

So perhaps it's a stalemate
Between Humans and Germs
Forever a part of each other
That's just how the World turns

— Written by RayRay
4/22/20 ©

Irvin R. Brookstein

SOS SOS

We used to be called
The Land of the Free
Once the Home of the Brave
Be all we can be

We used to meet up
At the Church or the Beach
Now you risk an arrest
If you Surf or you Preach

We use to shake hands
Give a pat on the back
Now any touch by a Friend
May be called an assault or attack

There once was an elevator
Packed to the brim
Now we must all take the stairs
You either die or suck wind

There once was a Dance
Or lips we could kiss
Forget having sex
Population growth no longer exists

We can't get on a Plane
Or take a seat on a bus
An Uber or Taxi is out
Run or walk, is a must

We once had a job
Took pride in our work
But don't worry at all
We all live on a Government perk

When the Virus is tamed
And the damage is done
We'll never need a vaccine
Once we are under their thumb

— *Written by RayRay*
5/1/20 ©

Irvin R. Brookstein

Safety First

So where is this all going
Their strategy's unfurled
No more human contact
Behold your new virtual world

At your business Zoom meetings
You'll be split on a screen
So off with your trousers
Your privates will barely be seen

Church services fading
Perhaps God will forgive
Parks are fenced off
It's our new way to live

Highways are empty
Emissions are down
It's progress they claim
Your Town Square, a Ghost town

All in the name
Of Government control
Do you remember the Constitution?
Good grief, It's been flushed down the bowl

Driverless vehicles
Deliver your meals
Tho we're allowed to do take out
If it's drive-thru that appeals

The virus came and it conquered
As if it were planned
Don't bother protesting
Even that has been banned

So welcome to Fascism
We let it seep in
We sacrificed our Freedom
For a diaper and a huge safety pin

— *Written by RayRay*
5/2/20 ©

Irvin R. Brookstein

Live Free or Die

They're commandeering buildings
So the homeless have a home
Now the Government's your concierge
The Ritz Carlton's not alone

You opened up your hair salon
Better get down on your knees
Seven days within a cell
A scalping if you please

Tatoo Parlors are taboo
The Law will make a stink
Hook the owner by the wrists
Deny his right to put on ink

If you should turn age Sixty-five
You might never leave your home
Kiss goodbye the light of day
At least you've got a TV and a phone

Be careful when you walk the dog
Or push the baby stroller too
They've imposed, that swings are closed
Or off to Jail with you

They want the names of worshipers
Who came to Temple or a Church
For in God's name, it's sure inane
What's the heinous reason for their search?

It you feel no sense of urgency
When they take away your Rights
Welcome to Nazi Germany
They laid down without a fight

They must be made to understand
That Freedom resides with us
We need not prove this legal point
To tyrants we can't trust

— *Written by RayRay*
5/7/20 ©

Irvin R. Brookstein

The Prophecy

Evil lurks at every corner
Directly or a bit obtuse
Everyday they test his psyche
But he's immune to their abuse

They've come at him from every angle
Like a VR MASK or X-Box game
But he's been shielded like a Knight in armor
No Earthly sword can pierce his frame

Sabotage and misinformation
Truthful reporting disappeared
Judges show their tainted mission
Tossing Justice on its rear

Impeachment trials and House subpoenas
Came at him like rabid dogs
They chomped with canines at his torso
But he's THE REBEL WITH OUR CAUSE

They sent a Virus licked by Satan
It's ground the World to a screeching halt
Jobs were lost and families hungered
Stay at home and lock the vault

But darkness can not last forever
Freedom can't ever be contained
Patriots who've become the targets
Will be pardoned in His Holy Name

It makes one wonder where he came from
Was he in fact, a Prophecy?
Was God in search of such a leader
With divine initials D J T?

He's foiled the Kings of Global Structure
He'll capture those who hatched the plot
Ropes or Needles will become their choices
Restoring Hope in all we've got

— *Written by RayRay*
5/15/20 ©

Irvin R. Brookstein

Contact Tracers

You shouldn't be surprised
When they knock upon your door
It's a community "Contact Tracer"
Sent along to find out more

They've been hired by Big Brother
To track your COVID-19 Sneeze
You can kiss good-bye your privacy
Tracking coughs and your disease

It could be your Friend or Neighbor
You must tell them where you ate
Give them names and their home numbers
iPhone input seals your fate

It Reminds me of the Nazis
They made you snitch upon your friend
Obscene to locate many Jews
Who were murdered in the end

Their ID may look so fancy
Match their shirt of Color Brown
You'll be commanded to obey them
Or else you'll be going Down

The First Term, Through Poetry

They will say their job is Noble
Stop infections in their track
Never mind our loss of Liberty
Once it's gone it won't come back

They've convinced a homegrown army
While the Congress funds their fee
Thirty million people out of work
Perfect for a Health Cop Tracking Spree

Next time they may bring needles
To Vaccinate you on the spot
While you thought UPS™ was at the door
TRUST ME ...IT WAS NOT

— Written by RayRay
5/16/20 ©

Backlash is a Bitch

They burned down inner cities
To soothe their burning itch
Shattered dreams are such a pity
But Backlash is a Bitch

Some Cops have been a kneelin
Those cowards flipped the switch
We the People are just reelin
Oh yes Backlash is a bitch

The Rinos are revealin
Just who they're gonna pitch
Beware of votes that they'll be stealin
Though Backlash is a Bitch

The Mayors are a pleadin
So money keeps them rich
They left their City cut and bleedin
Heck Backlash is a Bitch

They want Police defunded
But there is just one glitch
Personal security will still be needed
Oh Backlash is a Bitch

The First Term, Through Poetry

Gloves and masks depleted
We tossed them in a ditch
Social distancing defeated
Yes Backlash is a bitch

It's time we turned the page
For months we followed script
The Republic must be saved
Show them Backlash is a Bitch

One Hundred fifty days and counting
Deplorables will make it stick
Biden's opposition's mounting
By God Our vote will sink the Bitch

— *Written by RayRay*
6/7/20 ©

Irvin R. Brookstein

Save our Country

We can't continue to appease them
It's become a National Shame
Governors have abandoned ship
Poof..their City's up in flames

Shops are being looted
Buildings burning down
City council heads are in the sand
Not one citizen's safe and sound

The streets are overtaken
Life and Liberty is at risk
When the Sun goes down in your hometown
There's no one to resist

Chaos sown by Anarchists
We've let them have their way
This is no longer about a death protest
Of course the Media will never say

It's time to bring the Infantry
Our own soil we must defend
We're at War within our shores
Which many fail to comprehend

Collusion was a hoax
Impeachment was a bust
A Virus took us to the brink
But Fighting insurrection is a must

By God..this is America
We must fight to keep it free
We can't bow to thugs and terrorists
They're more deadly than the disease

So load up with your Ammo
Protect the ones you Love
We can count on Trump to lead the charge
With the help from God above

— *Written by RayRay*
6/2/20 ©

Irvin R. Brookstein

I "Woke" in 2020

I feel like Rip Van Winkle
Woke after twenty years
Everything I knew before
It's no longer as it appears

Men in Blue were often called
When things got out of hand
Now they're dodging Molotovs
Tossed by hooded 'kerchief bands

We would stand and cross our heart
When our Anthem would be sung
Now players pound their knee to ground
And fans no longer come

Everybody had a job
Payday's were so sweet
Now millions wallow out of work
Without enough to eat

People used to hug and kiss
Love was all around
Now mask and gloves shield us from love
Leaving saddened eyes and muffled sound

Attending College was a dream
We achieved an educated voice
If you don't opine, the party line
They'll peer shame you for your choice

I took a snooze for twenty years
Do you remember Y2K
I guess Civilization didn't end
But I'm not so sure today

Now I'm Woke, I better vote
When November comes along
Someone better Wake America
They've been sleeping far too long

— Written by RayRay
6/30/20 ©

Cancelling America

I thought it was a Joke
Someone's pulling at my leg
They're canceling America?
No more Blue Moon in a keg?

They're cancelling the Redskins
Oklahoma's given back
Next will be the WhiteHouse
No doubt to the color Black

There's Goya paranoia
Frijoles and White Rice
Boycott their brand, throughout the land
Because he said that Trump was nice

They're cancelling Deplorables
And Suppressing what we say
God Forbid should Biden win
They're gonna make us pay

They'll tear down every statue
They'll decide that they'd done wrong
Judgment through a sordid current view
The Eyes of History say so long

They'll be cancelling our Culture
They'll say everything must go
400 years of blood, sweat and tears
If we let Leftists run the show

It's time we stood up to this crap
Raise our fists and load our gun
Show these bullies that it's time
To blow cancellation to Kingdom come

I pledge that I'll keep writing
I will never spare this pen
I know that God will say to me
Ray, this chance may never come again

— *Written by RayRay*
7/11/20 ©

Irvin R. Brookstein

"No Right to Bare Arms"

It won't be very long
Before we're losing every Fight
Even though they're all God Given
They'll make us sacrifice each Right

It started with the Right to Speak
We no longer have our say
Because someone got offended
It's the speaker who must pay

They took away our rifles
So we can't protect our kin
They care more about the looters
For what we own's a mortal sin

They've been trafficking our children
They're aborting the pre-born
They claim only Black Lives Matter
It's a Progressive Perfect Storm

You may think that this wont happen
I sure no one would place Bets
Finally everyone is outraged
When they prohibit household Pets

The First Term, Through Poetry

Say good bye to Cats and Dogs
No more poopeeing in the Street
Watch the Congressmen and Women feast
While We The People barely eat

Welcome to the Depraved New World
COVID Masks cover smiles of teeth
Bare Arms and Skin never seen again
Sharia men police the street

They took a little more each day
We hardly noticed when
This better rock you to your feet
It's the beginning of the end

— Written by RayRay
7/20/20 ©

Irvin R. Brookstein

What's in a Name?

The word is so cheap
It's so easy to use
No Proof is required
You've got nothing to lose

When you're in doubt
If you've run out of words
Lay down a mine field
Who cares if it's absurd

Some call it ole faithful
Designed as a low blow
There's no way to defend it
Just so you know

They hope that it gets you
To frame a response
To put you on the defensive
A place nobody wants

You've lived a good life
Never meant anyone harm
But all in an instant
They rang the alarm

The First Term, Through Poetry

Accuse you of something
Who cares if it's true
The label's demeaning
So abusive to you

So how do you fight it?
Without losing your pride
Perhaps it's best to ignore it
In that moment decide

Calling someone a Racist
Is a cowardly act
Just hold up a mirror
Give them their reflection right back

— *Written by RayRay*
7/23/20 ©

Irvin R. Brookstein

The Black Widow

She fits their Bill on Paper
The Left is all aglow
She'll weave right to the Summit
With spinnerets to and fro

Biden's been a hiding
He knows his end is close at hand
If by chance, he wins the dance
His neck is where her fangs will land

She'd leave the Country Widowed
She's a Marxist to the core
Her web of deceit, is near complete
Like we've never seen before

They'll be healthcare for illegals
Porous walls will let them in
She fabricated Blackness
Exposed her Indian Jamaican skin

She's sure to strike with vengeance
Just ask Judge Kavanaugh
Vicious attacks give us a glimpse
Of what Conservatives have in store

They'll claim that she is moderate
But just you wait and see
Free speech and guns, unborn on the run
Christians forced to take a knee

Sleepy Joe won't even know
He's their puppet on a string
They'll Invoke the 25th Amendment
His Dementia's clearly what they'll sing

So beware of Kamala
Better check her gunny sack
She comes with tons of baggage
With a Red Dot on her back

— *Written by RayRay*
8/19/20 ©

God Bless Humanity

He's been absorbing all the hatred
More than any man can take
Not a moment ever lets up
Nor an exit to escape

No man lives without some sin
And yet they're casting stones
Taking deadly aim each day
Slinging sticks to break his bones

The Battle has been brewing
The Election's round the bend
One side wants to terminate
The other to defend

The Virus came and called his name
Along with his Mrs. too
We should thank the Grace of God
It has not infected you

Kind words appear to quell the fear
From folks we'd never thought
Expressions of humanity
Just like our parents taught

The First Term, Through Poetry

It's time our Nation starts to heal
Let the Candidates seize the day
Let Love lead to acceptance
So hatred fades away

The past four years, so full of fears
Friends and family have been lost
Live and let live, learn to forgive
Life's too short to bear this cost

— *Written by RayRay*
10/3/20 ©

Courting Justice

The Left's been spewing insults
They tried as best they could
They failed stalling Trump's selection
Claiming Amy was no good

They couldn't crack her brilliance
Nor attack her Motherhood
She's a "Fighting Irish" Catholic
The Rule of Law's well understood

The Senate did their duty
Republicans had their way
Fifty-two to Forty-eight
That Nuclear option on display

They hurried to the WhiteHouse
Confirmed her in the dark of night
Clarence Thomas swore her in
Now the Bench can break a tie

Liberal fears reach a crescendo
There's so much they could lose
Fifty years of SCOTUS progress
They see going down the tubes

The First Term, Through Poetry

Now the Left is plotting
That they must pack the Bench
They must offset Amy, Neil and Brett
It's a political Monkey Wrench

Obamacare's up in the air
Ballot deadlines are defined
Who will win to my chagrin
I can't predict this time

Let's welcome Justice Amy
Generations in her hand
May the Constitution stand up tall
Above our precious land

— *Written by RayRay*
10/27/20 ©

The Curse Of 2020

Four years ago
A raging battle began
A Woman in the White House
Was the Democrat's game plan

But lightning from Heaven
Struck with shock and with awe
A bolt struck the Electoral College
Left a flood of tears on the Floor

He raised up his hand
On a Bible was sworn
Barely nineteen hours later
An Impeachment was born

We watched the Media throttle
Every success which he made
Whether peace in the Middle-East
Covid-19 or tariffs on trade

2020 came quickly
Now the Election's at hand
Joe Biden's their Savior
Ousting Trump is what's planned

The First Term, Through Poetry

It appeared Trump was heading
To a White Housing win
Then they halted the counting
Let Battleground mail-in-ballots slip in

We watched Wisconsin and Michigan
Flip over to Blue
Arizona called early
Could ballot dumping be true?

Legal challenges are filed
No clear winner declared
Just who is the President
Is now way up in the air

Will it end up with SCOTUS?
I think that's a sure bet
I believe that the new sitting Justice
Won't recuse herself yet

The influence of COVID
Infected this Presidential Race
Who would have thought that a virus
Would turn this Election right on its face

— *Written by RayRay*
10/5/20 ©

www.ingramcontent.com/pod-product-compliance
Lightning Source LLC
Chambersburg PA
CBHW070727160426
43192CB00009B/1339